SEASONS
of
LOUISIANA

Chef Peter Sclafani

"It's one thing you aspire to: someday, you'll be able to write a book."

CHEF THOMAS KELLER

Published by Chef Peter Sclafani
18811 Highland Road
Baton Rouge, Louisiana 70809

Created and produced by Xdesign, Inc.
8530 Quarters Lake Road
Baton Rouge, Louisiana 70809
www.thinkx.net

Printed by TriStar Graphics Group, Inc.
www.tristargraphics.com

www.chefpetersclafani.com
www.ruffinosrestaurant.com

Cover and Book Design: Xdesign, Inc.
Creative Direction: Hunter Territo, Xdesign, Inc.
Art Direction & Design: Tiffanie Pitre, Xdesign, Inc.
Photography by: Collin Richie and Frank McMains, Assisted by Marianne and Steve Sabrier

ISBN # 978-0-615-89515-4

Special Note for Businesses and Schools
Seasons of Louisiana is available at quantity discounts with bulk purchase for educational, business,
or sales promotional use. For more information please email Hunter Territo at hunter@thinkx.net.

DEDICATION

To my wife, Michelle, whose selfless support has enabled
me to live my dream.

To my children, Peter IV and Katherine, who are the reasons
I passionately pursue the very best for them.

FOREWARD *by* CHEF JOHN FOLSE

FOREWARD

Peter Sclafani is what I call a Louisiana "heritage chef," which is a culinary breed all its own. Not only did he grow up in a great Italian family; he grew up in a great Italian restaurant family. His grandfather, also named Peter, established Sclafani's, a great Mid City restaurant on Palmyra Street in New Orleans, until he outgrew the space and relocated to Causeway Boulevard in the late 1950s. It was only natural that Peter followed in his grandfather's footsteps as well as his dad and uncle, who ran Sclafani's together until the late 1960s.

Being a seasoned chef, I have had the privilege of knowing Peter for many years now and have watched him grow into the exceptional culinarian, restaurateur and entrepreneur that he is. Deeply rooted in Louisiana tradition, his passion for cooking runs in his DNA.

I love this first cookbook of Peter's, *Seasons of Louisiana,* because it speaks to the heart of every cook, and certainly every Louisianian. While we understand that most people live by the traditional spring, summer, winter, fall, Louisiana has diverse seasons all her own: shrimp season, crab season, crawfish season, hunting season, and Peter captures each of these seasons and more with his richly developed recipes. While all of his dishes are exceptional, I would love to sink my teeth into his Rabbit Ragu, Tuna Puttanesca Pasta or have a slice of his mile-high Crawfish Cheesecake. Even if I were not a chef, I could easily work my way through his clear and precise recipes that are not overly complicated for the home cook who just wants to prepare a great plate of food.

Peter has a passion for cooking that can only be matched by his philanthropic and professional work. He is a founding board member of the Baton Rouge Epicurean Society, the recipient of the Louisiana Restaurant Association's prestigious "Restaurateur of the Year Award" and a tireless supporter of the Sister Dulce Foundation.

As a leading chef in the state of Louisiana, he has also had a tremendous influence on young culinary minds. Peter continues to influence (inspire) the American palate one ladle of Louisiana Crawfish & Asparagus Bisque at a time. There is no shortage of cookbooks in our literary landscape, and Louisiana chefs have certainly contributed their share to bookshelves, coffee tables and kitchen counters worldwide. But clear a little space, because your culinary library will be incomplete without the fabulous new contribution by Chef Peter Sclafani.

It is a distinct privilege to have written the foreword to this exceptional new cookbook, *Seasons of Louisiana,* and wish Peter many future successes through every season of his life.

TABLE *of* CONTENTS

SEASONS *of* LOUISIANA

INTRODUCTION

It's the dream of every Chef...to one day see a cookbook with your name on it. For the last 18 months, I have worked tirelessly, along with the outstanding team around me, to produce my first cookbook. Even though the production process consumed the better part of the last year and a half, the inspiration began decades ago at the onset of my culinary career. As I said, this is every Chef's dream. Thank you for making my dream come true.

The process began at "Table 12" in Ruffino's Restaurant in Baton Rouge. My team and I were having one of our weekly meetings and that's when I decided to stop dreaming and finally get started on making my first printed cookbook a reality.

As we batted around a long list of potential recipes, we also discussed what we liked about other cookbooks. For example, seasonal cooking has become very popular and lots of books arrange their recipes by Winter, Spring, Summer and Fall.

Many people joke that Louisiana only has two seasons. I beg to differ. Though our weather may not be the draw of the south, there's no debate that our food is the draw. When it comes to a meal, there's no doubt Louisiana celebrates many "seasons."

That was our "aha" moment, when we knew the title would be "Seasons of Louisiana." We never looked back after that.

When you think about it, nothing says it's football season like a pot of jambalaya. Nothing screams crawfish season like a roaring pot boiling with friends and family gathered in the backyard... And there's nothing like a cold batch of marinated crab claws to refresh your soul on a hot summer day.

Throughout the following pages, I share the philosophy that drives each of my restaurants: Serve great food from local producers that tells an amazing story. After all, it's not just the food that brings us together and creates wonderful memories. It's the stories.

Seasons of Louisiana is a snapshot in time of where I am as a Chef at this moment. I've even seen myself evolve throughout the creation of this cookbook. It's part of why I love being a Chef, because I'm constantly pushing the culinary envelope to create my next great recipe.

I am very proud to be a Louisianian, and I believe there's no place on Earth that produces more original, delicious and innovative food than Louisiana. As you go through and prepare the dishes highlighted in this book, I think you'll come to agree with me.

Again, thank you for being a part of making this dream come true. I hope you enjoy all the wonderful meals our great state has to offer.

SHRIMP SEASON

Some of the most fun, and yet most grueling work I've ever done on a boat was shrimping. I remember going out with my father, Pete, and my brother, Gino, on Lake Pontchartrain. After a long day on the boat, my dad would always make BBQ Shrimp Pasta the night we returned. It was well worth the effort.

Louisiana shrimping season typically runs from late spring to early winter; but shrimp can be found all year round since they freeze well and can be caught offshore.

When purchasing shrimp, I always insist they not be treated. Some shrimpers treat their shrimp with sodium tripolyphosphate which I find gives them a soapy taste. I recommend finding your local farmers market or a truck on the side of the road for the best shrimp. When it comes time to storing your fresh shrimp, it is best to use ice water rather than just ice on top.

Shrimp is another Louisiana ingredient that can be delicious whether boiled or fried, and everything in between. Pick up a couple of pounds of fresh shrimp, grab a crisp chardonnay and life is good.

SHRIMP & AVOCADO CROSTINI

Yields 32 Crostini

Boiled Shrimp:

2 gallons water

3 cups crab boil

2 lemons, halved

1 onion, quartered

5 cloves garlic

5 bay leaves

32 shrimp, shell on

Shrimp & Avocado Crostini:

4 avocados, peeled, seeded, and diced

juice of 1 lime

½ cup red onion, peeled and chopped

1 jalapeño pepper, seeded and diced

½ cup tomato, seeded and diced

2 tablespoons cilantro, chopped

1 tablespoon extra virgin olive oil

1 teaspoon sea salt

½ teaspoon fresh ground black pepper

32 boiled shrimp, peeled

1 loaf New Orleans style French bread

½ cup salted butter

For the Boiled Shrimp:

Bring the water and the remaining ingredients except the shrimp to a rolling boil. Cook for at least 5 minutes. Add the shrimp and turn off the heat. Let the shrimp soak for 15 minutes. Taste the shrimp to see if they have absorbed enough flavor. Let them soak longer if needed.

For the Shrimp & Avocado Crostini:

In a mixing bowl, toss the avocado with the lime juice. This will keep the avocado from oxidizing. Stir in the onion, jalapeño, tomato, cilantro, olive oil, salt, and pepper. Mix well trying to keep the integrity of each ingredient and not mash them.

Preheat the oven to 350° F. Slice the French bread into 32 ¼" slices. Brush each slice with melted butter. Place the sliced French bread on a sheet pan and bake for 5 minutes or until crisp and golden brown.

Place about 1 tablespoon of the avocado salsa on each crostini.

Top with a boiled shrimp.

SHRIMP CORN DOGS

Yields 24

1 ¼ cups yellow corn meal

1 ½ cups all purpose flour

1 ⅛ cups sugar

1 ½ tablespoons baking powder

½ teaspoon sea salt

½ teaspoon fresh ground white pepper

2 cups milk

2 eggs

24 large shrimp, peeled

2 tablespoons Creole seasoning *(page 166)*

24 bamboo skewers

mustard sauce *(page 171)*

Combine the corn meal, flour, sugar, baking powder, salt, and pepper in a mixing bowl and whisk to combine. In another mixing bowl, beat the eggs and whisk in the milk until well combined. Pour the wet ingredients into the dry ingredients and whisk until well combined. This should produce a wet smooth batter.

Skewer the shrimp (I use 16/20 headless, peeled) from the tail to the head keeping the shrimp as straight as possible. Once all your shrimp are skewered, season on all sides with Creole seasoning and dust in seasoned flour, shaking off all the excess.

Dip the shrimp head first into the batter until the shrimp is completely coated. Remove from the batter allowing the excess to drip off. I twirl the shrimp to even the batter.

Lower the shrimp head first into a fry basket that is set in a preheated fryer, holding on to the skewer. Allow to fry for 5 seconds before dropping. This should allow the batter to set so it does not stick to the basket.

When the first 6 shrimp are in the fryer, cover with another basket to keep the skewers submerged so they will brown evenly.

Cook until golden brown, about 2 minutes. Remove from the basket and allow to drain. Repeat with the remaining shrimp.

Serve with mustard sauce.

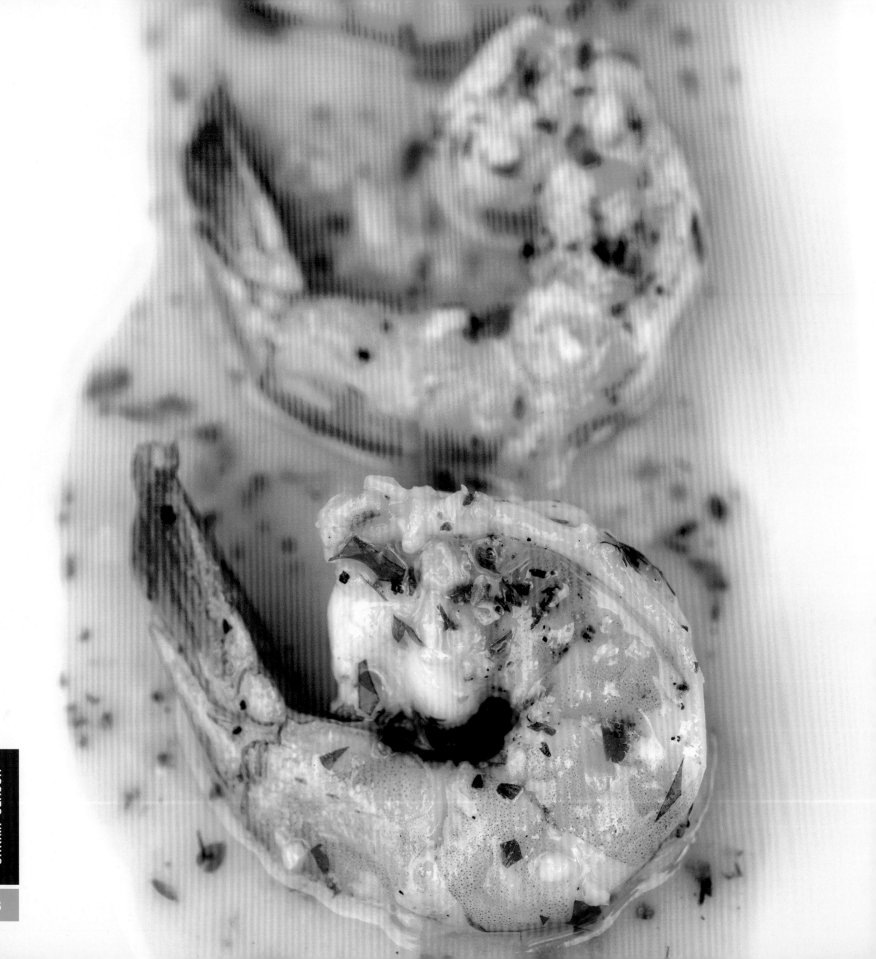

SHRIMP SCAMPI

Serves 2

1 pound unsalted butter, softened

2 tablespoons garlic, minced

3 tablespoons shallots, minced

½ cup fresh Italian parsley, chopped

2 teaspoons Herbsaint

1 ½ teaspoons sea salt

1 teaspoon fresh ground white pepper

12 jumbo shrimp *(about 16 shrimp per pound)*, peeled with tails left on and deveined

sea salt to taste

fresh ground black pepper to taste

juice of half a lemon

¼ cup white wine

French bread as accompaniment

CHEF'S NOTES

I love a versatile recipe. This dish uses a classic New Orleans bordelaise that combines the butter, garlic and lemon flavors that pair perfectly with so many items. This makes a great appetizer with some fresh French bread; but it also makes a great sauce for your favorite pasta. You can even use this to top steaks and fish.

To make the compound butter, blend together the butter, garlic, shallots, parsley, Herbsaint, salt, and pepper in a food processor until smooth.

Layout a sheet of plastic wrap. Spoon the butter along the side facing you, about 2" from the edge. Fold the end of the plastic wrap nearest you over the butter and continue rolling creating a 2" log of butter. Twist the ends closed.

Refrigerate or freeze until firm enough to slice. The butter will keep frozen for several weeks.

Heat a large skillet with the olive oil over medium-high heat.

Season the shrimp with salt and pepper, add the shrimp to the pan, and cook until the shrimp turn pink. Deglaze the pan with lemon juice and white wine and add 4 tablespoons of compound butter to the skillet.

Reduce the heat to a simmer and cook, shaking the skillet until the butter is emulsified.

Pour onto serving plates and serve with hot French bread.

BUTTERNUT SQUASH & SHRIMP BISQUE

Serves 16

1 stick butter

2 cups onions, peeled and chopped

1 cup celery, chopped

1 cup carrots, peeled and chopped

2 cups shrimp, peeled

1 tablespoon garlic, chopped

1 tablespoon Creole seasoning *(page 166)*

1 bay leaf

4 cups butternut squash,
peeled, seeded, and cut into 1" cubes

6 cups shrimp or chicken stock

½ teaspoon ground cumin

sea salt to taste

fresh ground black pepper to taste

2 cups heavy whipping cream

2 tablespoons honey

Optional:

1 cup sour cream

¼ cup heavy whipping cream

Melt the butter in a large stockpot over medium-high heat. Add the onions and cook for about 2 minutes until soft.

Add the celery and carrots and cook for about 5 minutes until soft. Add the butternut squash and cook for 10 additional minutes.

Stir in the shrimp, garlic, and Creole seasoning and cook for 5 minutes. Add the shrimp or chicken stock and bring to a boil. When it begins to boil, turn the heat down to a simmer and add the cumin. Cover and cook for about 20 minutes. The squash should easily mash against the side of the pot when pressed.

Purée with an immersion or regular blender. (*I recommend letting the soup cool before using a regular blender.*)

After the soup is puréed, stir in the cream and the honey.

If desired, mix the sour cream and heavy whipping cream and drizzle over the soup as a garnish.

Serve hot.

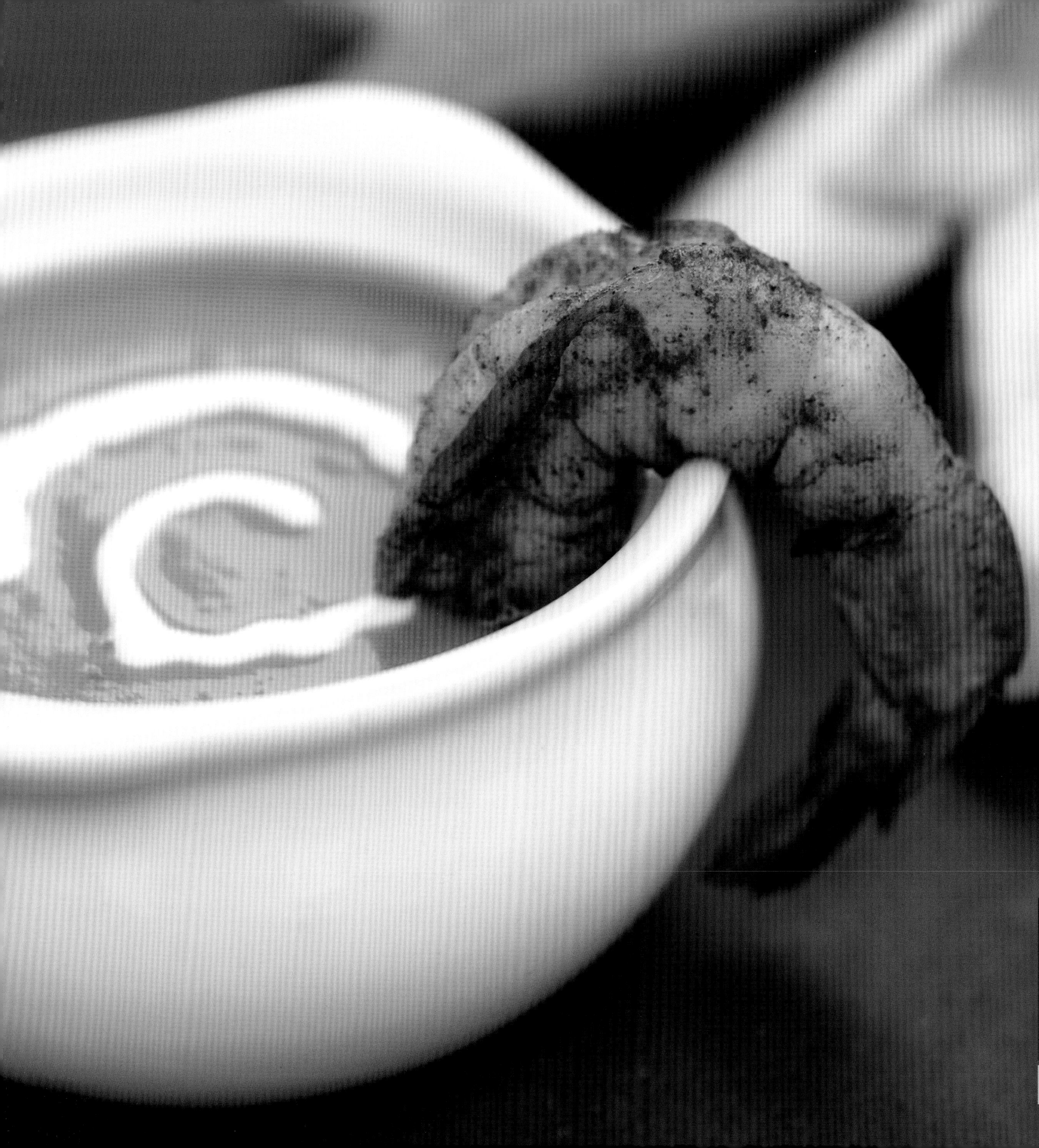

SHRIMP
SCLAFANI SALAD

→ *Yields 4 Small or 2 Large Salads* ←

2 cloves garlic

pinch sea salt

fresh ground black pepper to taste

2 anchovies

1 boiled egg, peeled

1 tablespoon balsamic vinegar

½ lemon, juiced

3 tablespoons olive oil

1 teaspoon Worcestershire

1 cup Creole remoulade *(page 171)*

1 Creole tomato, cut into wedges

½ red bell pepper, julienned

½ cup celery, chopped

8 boiled shrimp, peeled

8 Kalamata olives, pitted

4 green olives, halved

3 cups romaine or iceberg lettuce

½ teaspoon Louisiana hot sauce

CHEF'S NOTES

The Sclafani salad was created by my grandfather at his restaurant in Metairie, Restaurant Sclafani. He would always create the salad tableside to add to the guests' dining experience. It was a great alternative to a traditional Caesar salad. We even refer to it as the "Creole" Caesar salad.

In a large wooden salad bowl, add the garlic and salt.

With the tines of a fork, smash the garlic and salt into the sides of the bowl to form a paste. Add the anchovies and mash with the fork to form a paste. Add in the balsamic vinegar, lemon juice, olive oil, Worcestershire, and hot sauce and whisk with the fork. Add the egg and mash with the fork and blend into the dressing.

Add the Creole remoulade and blend well. Add the remaining ingredients and toss to coat. Divide all ingredients evenly onto chilled salad plates.

SHRIMP
BBQ SHRIMP PASTA

Serves 6

1 pound fettuccine

sea salt

1 tablespoon olive oil

36-40 large Gulf shrimp, peeled and deveined

4 ounces Budweiser beer

1 pound butter, cut into chips, at room temperature

1 tablespoon fresh ground black pepper

2 tablespoons Creole seasoning *(page 166)*

3 tablespoons Worcestershire sauce

2 tablespoons garlic, chopped

juice of 1 ½ lemons

2 tablespoons fresh rosemary, minced

CHEF'S NOTES

Here's an interesting culinary fact for your next trivia contest: BBQ Shrimp was originally created at Pascal's Manale Restaurant in uptown New Orleans. The recipe actually has nothing to do with BBQ or even a BBQ technique. It's called BBQ because of the color of the sauce. The sauce and shrimp are also great on just about any cut of beef, chicken, or pork. Enjoy this New Orleans classic.

Bring a large pot of water to a boil seasoned heavily with salt. It should taste like the sea. Add the fettuccine and stir. Cook according to package directions until al dente, soft but firm to the bite. Drain.

To make the compound butter, place the butter, black pepper, Creole seasoning, Worcestershire, garlic, lemon juice, and rosemary in a food processor. Blend until completely smooth and well blended.

Lay a sheet of plastic wrap on the counter and place the compound butter on the wrap and form into a log. Twist the ends to seal. Refrigerate.

Heat the olive oil in a sauté pan over medium-high heat.

Add the shrimp and cook until the shrimp begin to turn pink. Deglaze the pan with the beer. Lower the heat and whisk in the butter 1 piece at a time until it is creamy and emulsified.

Toss with the fettuccine and divide into 6 bowls.

15

SHRIMP & GRITS

Serves 4

Creamy Mascarpone Polenta:

2 cups chicken stock

1 cup heavy whipping cream

pinch nutmeg, ground

1 teaspoon sea salt

½ teaspoon fresh ground white pepper

¼ cup corn meal

¼ cup semolina

¼ cup Fontina cheese, grated

¼ cup Parmigiano-Reggiano, grated

½ cup Mascarpone cheese

Shrimp & Grits:

1 tablespoon olive oil

¼ cup tasso, diced

¼ cup onions, peeled and chopped

½ tablespoon garlic, chopped

24 jumbo shrimp, peeled and deveined
(tails on if desired)

½ cup tomatoes, peeled, seeded and diced

½ cup dry white wine

1 teaspoon fresh thyme, chopped

1 tablespoon Creole seasoning *(page 166)*

1 cup heavy whipping cream

1 tablespoon butter

1 tablespoon fresh Italian parsley, chopped

1 tablespoon green onions, sliced

2 cups creamy Mascarpone polenta *(above)*

For the Creamy Mascarpone Polenta:

In a large heavy pot over high heat combine the stock, cream, nutmeg, salt, and pepper and bring to a boil. While whisking, gradually add the corn meal and semolina. Continue to stir while cooking. When it starts to boil, reduce the heat to low and cook for 10 minutes. Stir in the cheeses until melted and remove from heat.

For the Shrimp & Grits:

In a sauté pan over medium-high heat, heat the olive oil and add the tasso and render for 1 minute.

Add the onions and cook for 2 minutes. Add the garlic and stir for 30 seconds to release the oils.

Stir in the shrimp and tomatoes until the shrimp just begin to turn pink. Deglaze with the white wine and add the thyme and Creole seasoning. Pour in the heavy cream and bring to a boil. Reduce the heat to a simmer. Add the butter, parsley, and green onions stirring to emulsify. Remove from heat. Taste the sauce for seasoning.

Place 1 cup of the polenta in the center of a plate and top each with 6 shrimp and the sauce.

CRAB CRUSTED SHRIMP

Serves 6

24 jumbo shrimp, butterflied and deveined *(tails remaining if desired)*

3 cups crabmeat dressing *(next page)*

1 tablespoon Creole seasoning *(page 166)*

6 tablespoons butter, melted

2 cups Choron sauce *(page 171)*

sea salt to taste

fresh ground black pepper to taste

3 cups crabmeat dressing *(next page)*

1 tablespoon Creole seasoning *(page 166)*

2 cups Choron sauce *(page 171)*

CHEF'S TIP

This was inspired by one of my grandfather's dishes, stuffed shrimp. While everyone is serving deep fried stuffed shrimp, I wanted to create a lighter version with the same flavors but without the batter and grease. We cook this dish in our wood burning brick oven, but your kitchen oven will do just fine.

Preheat oven to 350° F.

Divide the dressing into 24 1-ounce portions and roll into balls, slightly smaller than golf balls.

Season the shrimp with Creole seasoning.

Place a ball of stuffing on the bottom side of a shrimp and fold tail over the ball. Place the shrimp split side (vein side) down in a baking pan. Repeat with the remaining shrimp.

Drizzle the melted butter over the shrimp. Place in the oven uncovered and cook for 10-12 minutes or until the shrimp are cooked and the dressing is hot, basting once.

Divide onto 6 serving plates.

Spoon 1 tablespoon of Choron sauce over each shrimp.

CRABMEAT DRESSING

→⊣ Yields Stuffing for 24 Crab Crusted Shrimp ⊢←

1 pound jumbo lump crabmeat

2 cups milk

½ cup butter

1 cup onion, peeled and chopped

½ cup green bell pepper, seeded and chopped

½ cup celery, chopped

¼ cup green onion, sliced

½ tablespoon garlic, chopped

1 bay leaf

¼ cup flour

1 teaspoon dried oregano

1 teaspoon fresh thyme, chopped

¼ cup Romano cheese

¾ cups bread crumbs

2 eggs, lightly beaten

sea salt to taste

fresh ground black pepper to taste

Preheat oven to 350° F.

Place the milk in a saucepan over low heat. In a large stockpot, heat the butter over medium-high heat. Add the onions and cook for 2 minutes. Add the bell peppers and celery and cook another 2 minutes. Add the green onions, garlic, and bay leaf and cook for 1 minute to soften.

Stir in the flour to create a white roux. Do not let the roux brown. Slowly mix in the heated milk to form a Béchamel sauce. When the Béchamel begins to bubble, turn down the heat to a simmer.

Add the oregano and thyme. Season to taste with salt and pepper. Remove from heat and stir in the Romano cheese and bread crumbs. Fold in the beaten eggs.

Add the crabmeat and stir gently to mix but not to break up the lumps of crab. Pour into a casserole dish, and cover with film and foil, and bake for 30 minutes.

Remove the film and foil and cook 10 minutes longer.

Remove from oven and allow to cool before using.

CRAWFISH SEASON

Many of us Louisianians think it's the most wonderful time of year...winter ends, spring begins and Mardi Gras is just around the corner. Super Bowl Sunday is fast approaching and, although I'm sad to see the football season come to an end, I know my favorite food season is nearly here: Crawfish season!

Boiling crawfish, although hard work, is a labor of love for those of us born and raised in South Louisiana. Boiled crawfish are as much of a tradition in Louisiana as Mardi Gras, Jazz Fest, and parades.

Not only does my family celebrate Easter every year with a crawfish boil, but the Ruffino's summertime employee appreciation party features a midnight crawfish boil. My wife, Michelle, and I were even given a boil as a couples shower before our wedding. Teaching my son, Peter, how to prepare crawfish is a rite of passage for him as a young man growing up in Louisiana.

One side note: After crawfish boils, I like to save the heads to make stock that adds incredible flavor to several of my dishes.

However, boiling isn't the only way to enjoy crawfish. A package of fresh-peeled Louisiana crawfish tails is easy, convenient and delicious. Just remember they are already cooked, so you only have to warm them.

In the middle of crawfish season the price of peeled crawfish tails drops to make it an inexpensive alternative to jumbo lump crabmeat. During this time of year, I think of all the dishes in which I can substitute crawfish for crab. Once the season is over, I go back to using crab.

I have included several of my other favorite recipes here, including crawfish cheesecake. I know it sounds a little out there, but you won't believe how delicious it is. So, grab a six pack of your favorite Louisiana beer and get cooking. And most importantly, get eating!

CRAWFISH CHEESECAKE

Serves 12

Filling:

1 tablespoon olive oil

1 cup onions, peeled and chopped

1 tablespoon garlic, chopped

1 teaspoon sea salt

1 teaspoon fresh ground white pepper

1 ½ pounds cream cheese, at room temperature

4 eggs

1 ¼ cup Fontina cheese, grated

⅓ cup Parmesan cheese

⅓ cup Romano cheese

4 teaspoons lemon juice

½ cup green onions, sliced

1 pound fresh Louisiana crawfish tails

Crust:

1 cup plain bread crumbs

¾ cup Parmesan cheese, grated

½ cup unsalted butter, melted

1 tablespoon Creole seasoning *(page 166)*

Creole Meuniere sauce *(page 166)*

Hollandaise sauce *(page 171)*

Heat the olive oil in a large sauté pan over medium-high heat. Add the onions and cook until soft, about 5 minutes. Add the garlic and cook for an additional minute. Season the onion mixture with salt and pepper and mix well. Remove from heat and let cool.

Preheat the oven to 350° F.

For the crust, combine the bread crumbs, Parmesan, butter, and Creole seasoning in a mixing bowl. Pour into a 10" springform pan and press into bottom. Set aside.

In a food processor, blend the cream cheese until smooth. While the machine is running, add the eggs and blend until well incorporated.

Scrape this into a mixing bowl and stir in the onions mixture. Add the cheeses, lemon juice, green onions, and crawfish tails and mix well.

Pour into the prepared pan, cover with aluminum foil, and bake for 45 minutes or until set. Remove the foil and bake for 15 minutes longer. Remove from oven and allow to cool.

Cut into 12 slices and heat in a microwave or a preheated 250° oven until hot.

Serve with Creole Meuniere sauce and top with Hollandaise sauce.

CRAWFISH BEIGNETS

Yields 36 Beignets

2 large eggs

1 pound fresh Louisiana crawfish tails

1 tablespoon Creole seasoning *(page 166)*

¼ cup red bell peppers, seeded and diced

¼ cup green onions, sliced

1 tablespoon fresh Italian parsley, chopped

1 tablespoon garlic, minced

1 teaspoon fine sea salt

1 ½ cups all-purpose flour

1 teaspoon baking powder

½ cup Abita™ Amber beer

2 tablespoons Creole seasoning *(page 166)*

CHEF'S NOTES

Leave the powdered sugar in the pantry for this classic beignet recipe and bring it to the savory side for a great appetizer. Substitute crab, fish or shrimp to give it your own twist. I like to make a few dipping sauces for guests, especially green onion, Creole remoulade sauce or even truffled ranch. You can find these sauce recipes in the "lagniappe" chapter.

Preheat the fryer to 350° F.

In a large bowl whisk the eggs until frothy. Add the crawfish to the eggs and season with Creole seasoning. Stir in the bell peppers, green onions, parsley, garlic, salt, flour, baking powder, and milk, and stir until it has the consistency of wet dough.

When the oil is hot, drop large spoonfuls of beignet batter *(I use a small scoop)* and fry until golden brown and crispy, for about 3 minutes. Do this in batches to avoid overcrowding. Drain the beignets on paper towels. Season with some Creole seasoning.

Serve with Green Onion dipping sauce *(page 170)* for dipping.

CRAWFISH CAKES

⊢ Serves 12 as Appetizer or 6 as Entrée ⊢

2 tablespoons butter

1 cup onion, peeled and chopped

½ cup celery, chopped

¼ cup red bell pepper, seeded and chopped

1 tablespoon garlic, minced

3 cups fresh Louisiana crawfish tails

¼ cup green onions, sliced

2 tablespoons fresh Italian parsley, chopped

¼ cup Parmesan cheese, grated

2 teaspoons fresh thyme

3 tablespoons Creole mustard

juice of 1 fresh lemon

½ cup mayonnaise

1 tablespoon Old Bay seasoning

1 tablespoon Worcestershire sauce

1 teaspoon Louisiana hot sauce

2 teaspoons sea salt

1 teaspoon fresh ground black pepper

2 eggs

¾ cups dried Panko bread crumbs

¼ cup all-purpose flour

1 tablespoon Creole seasoning *(page 166)*

¼ cup olive oil

Creole remoulade *(page 171)*

CHEF'S NOTES

My crawfish cake recipe is a classic. You can even use the mixture as a stuffing with any type of fish or chicken. When crawfish are out of season, I like to substitute fresh crabmeat. If you desire a crawfish cake with more crunch, simply batter with Panko and fry.

Melt butter in a small sauté pan over medium heat. Add onions and cook for 2 minutes. Add the celery and bell peppers and cook about 3 minutes more. Add the garlic and cook for an additional minute. Cool for 5 minutes.

In a large mixing bowl, combine the crawfish, green onions, parsley, Parmesan, thyme, mustard, lemon juice, mayonnaise, Old Bay seasoning, Worcestershire, hot sauce, salt, and pepper together. Stir in the vegetable mixture then fold in the bread crumbs.

Divide combined mixture into 10 equal portions and form into 1-inch thick round patties.

In a shallow bowl, combine the flour and Creole seasoning. Dredge the crawfish cakes in the seasoned flour, tapping off excess.

In a large sauté pan, heat oil over medium-high heat.

Gently lay the cakes, 3 to 4 at a time, and pan fry until lightly golden, about 4 minutes on each side. Repeat with remaining cakes.

Serve with Creole remoulade.

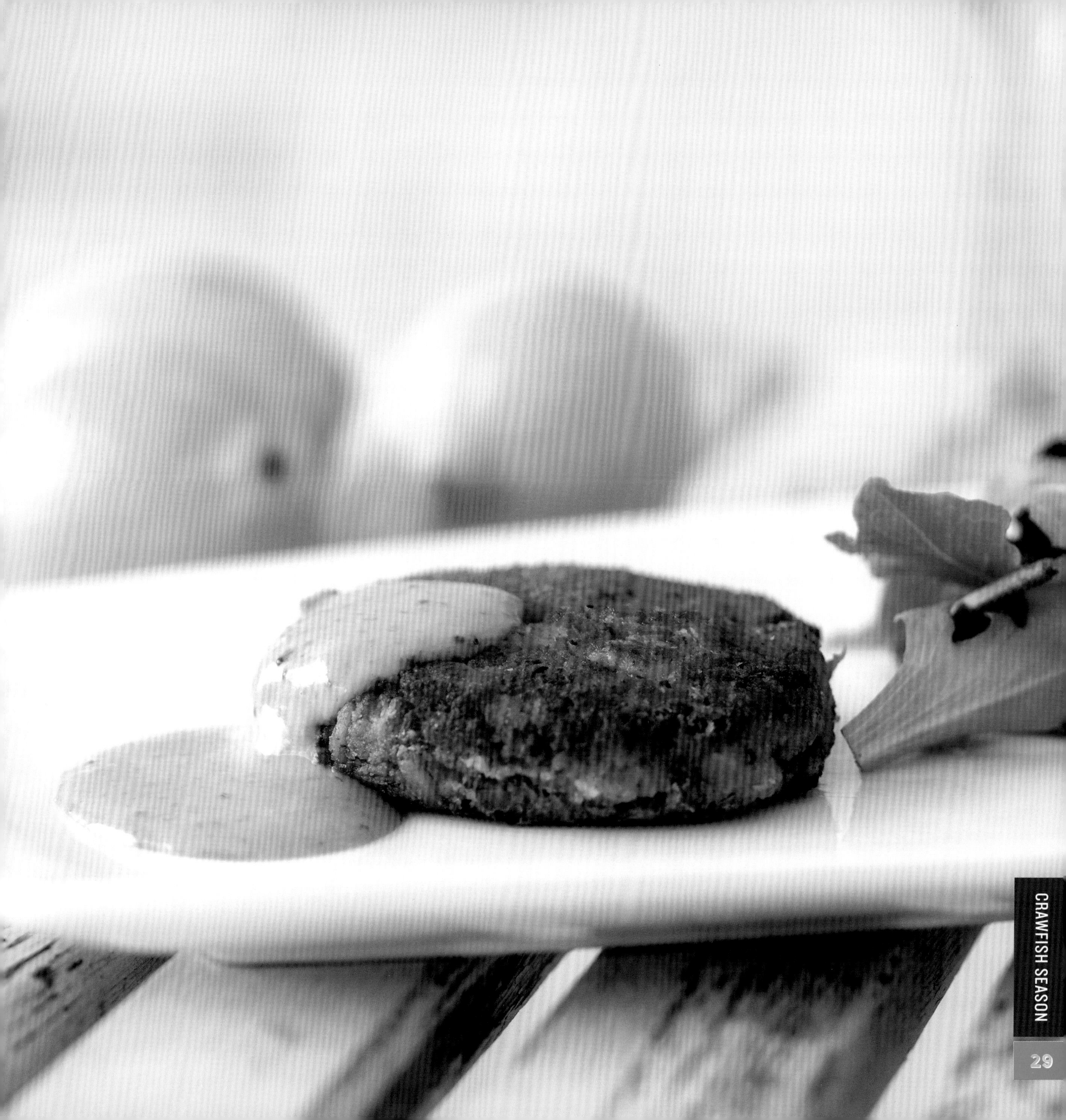

CRAWFISH & ASPARAGUS SOUP

Serves 12

2 bunches asparagus

1 cup unsalted butter

1 cup onions, peeled and chopped

½ cup celery, chopped

½ cup red bell pepper, seeded and chopped

1 tablespoon garlic, minced

1 cup flour

pinch nutmeg

2 ½ quarts crawfish stock
(chicken or seafood stock can be substituted)

1 cup tomatoes, peeled, seeded and diced

1 tablespoon fresh thyme
(1 ½ teaspoons if dried)

1 bay leaf

1 tablespoon Creole seasoning *(page 166)*

1 teaspoon sea salt

½ teaspoon fresh ground black pepper

¼ teaspoon cayenne pepper, ground

2 cups heavy whipping cream

2 pounds fresh Louisiana crawfish tails

¼ cup fresh Italian parsley, chopped

½ cup green onions, sliced

CHEF'S NOTES

This recipe is inspired by a dish prepared by my good friend and fellow chef, Chef John Folse, at his restaurant, Lafitte's Landing, located at the Bittersweet Plantation in Donaldsonville, Louisiana.

Cut the asparagus 5" from the tip. Place the asparagus bottoms in a stockpot with the crawfish stock and bring to a boil. Reduce the heat to a simmer. Cut the remaining asparagus tops into ½" pieces. Set aside.

Melt the butter in a large stockpot over medium-high heat. Add the onions and cook for 2 minutes. Add the celery and bell peppers and cook for 2 more minutes. Stir in the garlic and cook for 1 minute more.

Incorporate the flour and nutmeg while stirring to make a white roux. Cook for 2 minutes without adding any color to the roux. Slowly add in the crawfish and asparagus stock while whisking. Add the tomatoes, thyme, bay leaf, Creole seasoning, salt, and both peppers and bring to a boil. Reduce the heat and simmer for 20 minutes.

Add the asparagus tips, cream, and crawfish tails, and simmer for 5 minutes longer. Taste for seasoning.

Garnish with parsley and green onions when serving.

POPCORN CRAWFISH SALAD

with Creole Honey Mustard Vinaigrette

Serves 4

1 teaspoon garlic, minced

¼ cup Steen's cane vinegar

1 tablespoon Dijon mustard

1 tablespoon Creole mustard

6 tablespoons honey

1 cup olive oil

sea salt to taste

fresh ground black pepper

1 egg

1 cup milk

Creole seasoning *(page 166)*

1 pound fresh Louisiana crawfish tails

1 cup corn flour

1 cup masa harina
(a corn flour used to make tortillas)

8 cups baby greens

½ cup red onions, peeled and sliced

½ cup red bell pepper, seeded and julienned

In a small container, combine the garlic, cane vinegar, Dijon, Creole mustard, honey, and olive oil. Blend with an immersion blender, adjust the seasoning with salt and pepper, and blend again.

Heat a deep fryer to 350° F.

In a small container, whisk the egg and milk. Season the crawfish tails with about 2 tablespoons of Creole seasoning. In a small container mix the corn flour, masa, and 1 tablespoon Creole seasoning.

Add the crawfish to the egg wash then remove the crawfish and add to the corn flour mixture. Coat well and remove the crawfish, shaking off any excess, and place in the fryer. Fry for 2 minutes. Remove from the fryer and allow to drain on a plate lined with paper towels.

In a large mixing bowl, toss the greens, red onions, and bell peppers with the vinaigrette. Divide onto 4 plates. Divide the crawfish on top of the greens.

CRAWFISH & FAVA BEAN RISOTTO

Serves 6

6 cups crawfish stock, or more as needed
(chicken or seafood stock can be substituted)

2 tablespoons olive oil

2 tablespoons butter

1 medium onion, small dice

1 tablespoon garlic, minced

1 pound Arborio rice

1 cup white wine

1 pound fresh Louisiana crawfish tails

1 cups of fresh fava beans, removed from pods,
blanched and outer skin removed

½ cup freshly grated Parmesan cheese

¼ cup heavy whipping cream

2 tablespoons butter

sea salt to taste

fresh ground black pepper to taste

CHEF'S NOTES

Growing up as a Sicilian Catholic in Louisiana, my family always participated in the celebration of St. Joseph, who is commonly known as the patron saint of Sicily. Every spring during Lent, my family would cook for St. Joseph's Altar. In the Middle Ages, Sicilians prayed to St. Joseph to prevent a famine due to the severe drought at the time. The rain finally came and the community produced a large altar to honor St. Joseph for answering their prayers. The rain helped bring a plentiful fava bean crop that saved the Sicilians from starvation, which is why I always carry a fava bean in my pocket for good luck. I always say "When I peel fava beans, I'm doing penance."

Heat the stock in a stockpot to a boil then reduce heat to a simmer.

Meanwhile, heat the olive oil and butter in a Dutch oven over medium-high heat and sauté the onion until transparent, about 5 minutes. Add the garlic and stir for 1 minute. Stir in rice to coat with oil, about 1 minute. Stir in the white wine, bring to a boil then reduce heat to a simmer. Cook until the wine has been absorbed.

Add simmering stock 1 cup at a time, stirring constantly. Wait for the liquid to be absorbed before adding more stock. Continue adding stock until the rice is almost tender to bite.

Add crawfish and fava beans and cook 5 minutes longer. Rice should be tender but not chalky. Remove from heat; stir in cheese, cream, butter, salt, and pepper.

Divide into 6 bowls and serve immediately.

CRAWFISH MAC & CHEESE

Serves 8 as Appetizer or 4 as Entrée

4 ounces cream cheese

2 cups heavy whipping cream

1 pound elbow pasta, shells, or mezze rigatoni

¼ cup green onions, sliced thin

2 tablespoons fresh Italian parsley, chopped

2 pounds fresh Louisiana crawfish tails

1 cup Fontina cheese, shredded

1 cup Gruyere, shredded

sea salt to taste

fresh ground black pepper to taste

½ cup Panko bread crumbs

½ cup Parmigiano-Reggiano, grated

1 tablespoon white truffle oil

1 teaspoon Creole seasoning *(page 166)*

Preheat the oven to 350° F.

In a mixing bowl, whisk together the cream cheese and heavy cream and blend until smooth.

Cook the pasta in plenty of boiling salted water until al dente. Drain well. Pour the hot pasta into the bowl with the cream cheese and cream. Add the green onions, parsley, crawfish tails, Fontina, Gruyere, salt, and pepper and mix until well blended.

In a small mixing bowl, blend the Panko bread crumbs, Parmigiano-Reggiano, truffle oil, and Creole seasoning.

Divide the pasta into individual casseroles. Top with equal amounts of the bread crumb mixture. Bake until hot and the topping is crisp, about 12 - 15 minutes.

CRAWFISH MARIA

Serves 8

1 pound fettuccine
(any type of pasta can be substituted)

1 cup butter

1 cup onions, peeled and chopped

½ cup celery, chopped

½ cup red bell pepper, seeded and chopped

1 tablespoon garlic, minced

1 cup flour

½ cup white wine

2 quarts crawfish stock
(chicken or seafood stock can be substituted)

1 bay leaf

1 teaspoon oregano, dry

2 teaspoons fresh thyme, chopped

2 teaspoons fresh basil, chopped

1 tablespoon Creole seasoning *(page 166)*

2 teaspoons sea salt

1 teaspoon fresh ground black pepper

½ teaspoon white pepper, ground

¼ teaspoon cayenne pepper, ground

2 cups heavy whipping cream

2 pounds fresh Louisiana crawfish tails

½ cup green onions, sliced

¼ cup fresh Italian parsley, chopped

Bring a large stockpot of water to a boil. Add salt to make it taste like sea water. Cook the pasta until al dente, just cooked through but still firm. Drain and set aside.

Meanwhile, heat a large stockpot over medium-high heat and melt the butter. Sauté the onions for about 5 minutes. Add the celery and bell pepper and sauté an additional 5 minutes. Add the garlic and stir for 1 more minute.

Stir in the flour and cook to make a white roux. Add the white wine and whisk into the roux. Add the stock and continue to whisk to remove any lumps. Bring to a boil and reduce heat to a simmer.

Add the bay leaf, oregano, thyme, basil, Creole seasoning, salt, black pepper, white pepper, and cayenne pepper. Let simmer for 20 minutes.

Add the cream and taste for seasoning. Stir in the crawfish tails, green onions and parsley. Toss with the hot pasta and divide into 8 bowls and serve hot.

CRAWFISH STUFFED MIRLITON

Serves 12 as Appetizer or 6 as Entrée

6 mirliton

2 tablespoons olive oil

½ cup tasso, diced

1 cup onions, peeled and chopped

½ cup celery, chopped

½ cup red bell pepper, seeded and chopped

1 tablespoon garlic, minced

1 teaspoon fresh thyme, chopped

1 teaspoon fresh rosemary, chopped

1 tablespoon Creole seasoning *(page 166)*

1 cup crawfish stock
(chicken or seafood stock can be substituted)

½ cup heavy whipping cream

2 cups day old French bread, diced

1 cup Panko bread crumbs

½ cup Parmesan cheese

2 tablespoons green onions, sliced

2 tablespoons fresh Italian parsley, chopped

3 cups fresh Louisiana crawfish tails

sea salt, fresh ground black pepper,
and Louisiana hot sauce to taste

12 teaspoons butter

CHEF'S NOTES

My grandfather grew mirliton along his fence because they grow in vines every spring. A mirliton is also commonly referred to as a vegetable pear or chayote squash. It's a spring vegetable that comes from the squash family. If you can't find mirliton, or prefer another flavor, substitute eggplant or any other type of squash.

Bring a large stockpot of salted water to a boil. Add the mirliton and boil for 30 minutes or until fork tender. Drain and allow to cool.

Slice in half lengthwise and remove the seed and discard. Scoop out the flesh creating a mirliton shell. Reserve the pulp.

Preheat the oven to 350° F.

Heat the olive oil in a large pot over medium-high heat. Add the tasso and cook for 1 minute. Add the onions and cook for 2 minutes. Add the celery and bell peppers and cook 2 minutes more. Add the reserved mirliton pulp and cook until the liquid is evaporated. Add the garlic, thyme, rosemary, Creole seasoning, crawfish stock, and cream, and bring to a boil. Add the diced French bread and stir well. Cook for 5 minutes. Remove from heat.

Stir in half the bread crumbs, cheese, green onions, and parsley. Gently fold in the crawfish tails and adjust seasoning with salt, pepper, and hot sauce. Spoon the dressing into the mirliton shells, sprinkle the remaining bread crumbs over the stuffed mirliton, and top each with a teaspoon of butter.

Bake for 30 minutes or until hot and golden brown.

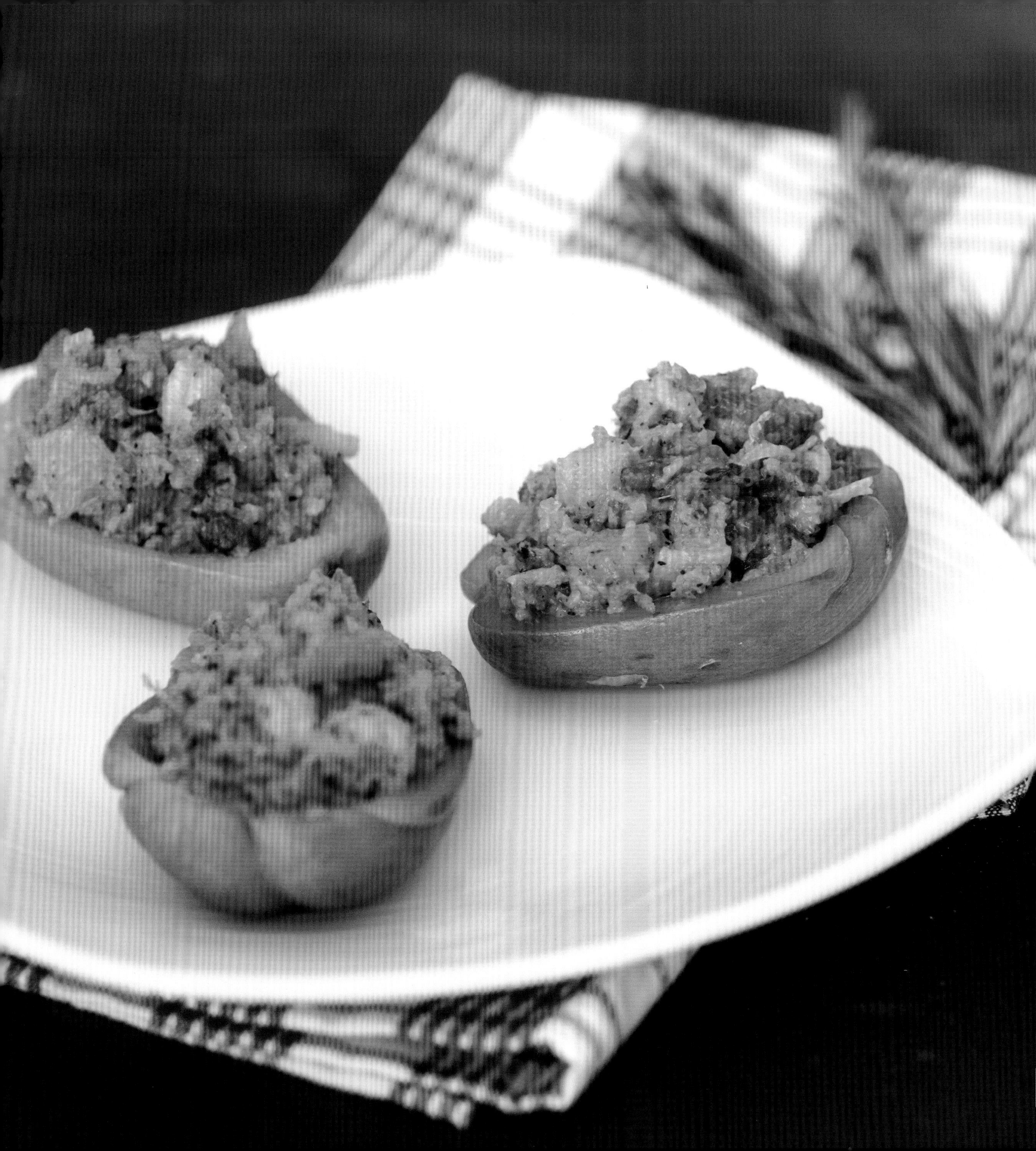

CRAB SEASON

Fresh crab is one of the most versatile ingredients Louisiana has to offer. One of my food philosophies is to use every part of an ingredient. In the following pages, you'll find recipes for crab claws and crab backs and every other type of meat found in a crab.

Jumbo lump crabmeat is the most expensive; however, you do get what you pay for. There are two jumbo lumps per crab and this is truly the best of the best. You then have lump crab meat, followed by backfin, which is more of a shredded style. The taste can be similar; however, the consistency becomes smaller and more shredded as you get less expensive. Marinated crab claws is the easiest recipe in the book; but I promise it doesn't lack in flavor.

Crab season typically runs from spring through summer. I can't write about crab season and not talk about a staple of seafood restaurants in Louisiana: soft shell crab. Soft shell crab typically has two seasons, the first around Mother's Day and then another around September.

Here are a couple of tips to consider as you begin cooking. First, crab meat purchased from the market is already fully cooked because the only way to extract the meat is by boiling the crabs. And second -- take it from a chef -- when in doubt, add crabmeat to the dish. It will always be better!

CRAB RAVIGOTE

Yields 36 Crostini

1 teaspoon dry mustard

1 tablespoon fresh lemon juice

1 cup mayonnaise

¼ cup red bell pepper, seeded and minced

¼ cup green bell pepper, seeded and minced

1 ½ tablespoons capers, drained and chopped

1 tablespoon fresh Italian parsley, minced

¼ cup Creole mustard

¼ cup prepared horseradish

½ teaspoon fresh ground black pepper

½ teaspoon tarragon

1 teaspoon Louisiana hot sauce

1 teaspoon Worcestershire sauce

1 pound fresh jumbo lump crabmeat

2 loaves New Orleans style French bread

1 cup salted butter, melted

CHEF'S NOTES

Derived from the term "Reinvigorate," ravigote is a classic sauce in the French cuisine. This is a great recipe to use for your leftover crab from a crab boil or another dish.

Preheat the oven to 350° F.

In a large mixing bowl, combine all the ingredients except the crabmeat, French bread, and butter and mix well.

Fold in the crabmeat being careful not to break up the lumps.

Slice the French bread into 36 ¼" slices. Brush each slice with melted butter.

Place the sliced French bread on a sheet pan and bake for 5 minutes or until crisp and golden brown.

Serve the crab ravigote on the toasted French Bread crostini.

Crab ravigote is also great on sliced Creole tomatoes or on fried green tomatoes.

HOT CRAB DIP

Yields ½ Gallon

1 quart heavy whipping cream

1 cup butter

½ cup onions, peeled and chopped

¼ cup celery, chopped

½ cup green onions, sliced

2 tablespoons garlic, minced

½ cup flour

¼ cup white wine

¼ cup lemon juice

1 teaspoon Louisiana hot sauce

1 cup grated Parmesan cheese

sea salt and cayenne pepper to taste

½ cup red bell pepper, diced

1 teaspoon fresh thyme, chopped

½ cup parsley, chopped

2 pounds jumbo lump crabmeat

1 pound claw crabmeat

2 loaves New Orleans style French bread

1 cup salted butter, melted

Heat heavy cream in a sauce pot until hot but not boiling. In a heavy bottom stockpot, melt the butter over medium-high heat. Add the onions, celery, green onions, and garlic and sauté until the onions begin to turn clear. Mix in the flour and stir to make a white roux. Be careful not to let the roux brown. Add the hot cream to the roux and stir well. Reduce heat to a simmer and add white wine, lemon juice, and hot sauce. Add Parmesan cheese stirring well so mixture does not scorch. Add red pepper, thyme, and parsley then fold in the crabmeat.

Preheat the oven to 350° F.

Slice the French bread into 64 ¼" slices. Brush each slice with melted butter. Place the sliced French bread on a sheet pan and bake for 5 minutes or until crisp and golden brown.

Serve the hot crab dip with the crostini.

MARINATED CRAB CLAWS

Serves 6-8

2 pounds crab fingers

¼ cup balsamic vinegar

¼ cup lemon juice

1 cup extra virgin olive oil

¼ cup red onions, peeled and chopped

¼ cup celery, chopped

¼ cup green onions, sliced

¼ cup fresh Italian parsley, chopped

2 teaspoons dried tarragon

2 teaspoons dried oregano

1 teaspoon fresh ground black pepper

1 ½ teaspoons sea salt

1 ½ teaspoons sugar

CHEF'S NOTES

This is the easiest recipe in the book! However, don't confuse its simplicity with lack of taste. Use this vinaigrette or any of your other favorite vinaigrette recipes for a delicious, quick-and-easy appetizer served cold. If you prefer warm crab claws, use the sauce from the shrimp scampi recipe on page 9 and sauté in a pan with claws.

Combine all ingredients and mix well. Let stand for at least 1 hour.

CORN & CRAB BISQUE

Makes 12 cups

2 quarts crab stock or chicken stock

12 ears of corn *(I prefer sweet white corn)*

1 cup butter

½ cup onion, peeled and chopped

1 teaspoon garlic

1 cup flour

2 teaspoons granulated crab boil

½ cup sugar

sea salt to taste

1 teaspoon ground white pepper

2 cups heavy whipping cream

1 pound jumbo lump crabmeat

1 bunch green onions, sliced

CHEF'S NOTES

I enjoy making trips with my brother Gino to the Baton Rouge Farmers Market to pick up fresh corn, green onions, and fresh Lake Pontchartrain crabmeat. These great ingredients are always available at a local farmers market in Louisiana. The sweetness of fresh corn in the summer pairs so well with the sweetness of the crab and butter. Add the cobs of the corn to the bisque for even more flavor.

Heat the crab or chicken stock in a sauce pot to a simmer.

Remove the kernels from the corn cobs by cutting them off the cobs with a knife. Using the back of the knife, scrape the cob to remove the milk of the corn. Set the kernels and scrapings aside and add the cobs to the stock.

In a large heavy bottomed stockpot, melt the butter over medium-high heat. Add the onions and garlic and cook for 1 minute. Add the corn and cook until it begins to get soft, about 5 minutes.

Stir in the flour, making a white roux. Do not let it brown. Whisk in the stock stirring to get out the lumps. Add the crab boil, sugar, sea salt and white pepper. Cook and stir until the soup thickens and just begins to boil. Reduce the heat to a simmer while stirring to make sure the flour does not scorch on the bottom of the pot. Continue to simmer for 10 minutes for the flavors to come together then remove from heat.

Stir in the heavy cream, crabmeat, and green onions. Serve hot.

CRAB & BRIE TART

Serves 4

1 stick butter

1 leek, sliced, white part only

¼ cup onions, peeled and chopped

¼ cup celery, chopped

1 cup sliced mushrooms

1 bay leaf

1 tablespoon garlic, minced

¼ cup flour

2 cups heavy whipping cream

2 tablespoons dry white wine

juice of 1 lemon

2 tablespoons brandy

1 pound crab claw meat

¼ pound Brie cheese, rind removed

¼ cup green onions, sliced

sea salt to taste

fresh ground black pepper to taste

4 large puff pastry shells

In a medium saucepan melt the butter over medium-high heat.

Add the leek, onions, celery, mushrooms, bay leaf, and garlic, and sauté until soft, about 5 minutes. Stir in the flour to make a white roux. Cook about 5 minutes to cook out the flour taste but not to color the roux.

Add the cream, white wine, and lemon juice, stirring to make a smooth sauce. Turn the heat to low and simmer for 10 minutes.

Add the Brie, brandy, claw meat, and green onions. Stir until the Brie has melted. Season to taste with salt and pepper. Remove from heat.

Heat the puff pastry according to package directions and spoon in the hot sauce allowing a small amount to spill out over one side.

CRABMEAT AGNOLOTTI

Yields 60 Agnolotti

1 ¾ cups "00" pasta flour
(all purpose can be substituted)

6 egg yolks

1 egg

1 ½ teaspoons olive oil

1 tablespoon water

1 teaspoon sea salt

semolina flour for dusting

1 tablespoon butter

1 tablespoon flour

1 cup cream, heated to a simmer

1 teaspoon sea salt

½ teaspoon ground white pepper

1 pound jumbo lump crab,
picked for shells

½ cup green onion, sliced

½ cup Parmigiano-Reggiano, grated

½ cup cracker crumbs

½ cup heavy whipping cream

4 tablespoons butter, softened

¼ cup Parmigiano-Reggiano, grated

½ teaspoon sea salt

½ teaspoon white pepper

In a food processor, place the egg yolks, egg, olive oil, milk, and salt. Process until well mixed. Add the flour and process until the dough just comes together. Dust a table with the semolina and knead the dough until it forms a ball. Wrap in plastic wrap and refrigerate for at least 30 minutes.

Melt the butter in a saucepan over medium-high heat. When the butter is melted, whisk in the flour. Cook for about 1 minute. Whisk in the hot cream. It should thicken immediately. Cook for 1 minute then remove from heat. Season with the salt and pepper. Fold in the crabmeat, green onions, cheese, and cracker meal. Set aside.

To make the agnolotti, cut the dough into 4 pieces. Remove 1 piece and wrap the remaining pieces. Flatten the dough and dust it with semolina.

Set the pasta machine to position 1. Pass the dough through, fold it in half and dust with semolina. Pass the dough through the machine again, repeating this process about 7 or 8 times. The dough should not be sticky and should feel silky.

Now turn the setting to 2 and pass through. Repeat, increasing the setting by 1 each time until you get to position 5. Dust the dough in semolina and run it 3 times through position 5.

Lay the dough on a lightly floured surface. Starting on the long side facing you, place a half tablespoon of stuffing in a ball ½" from the edge. Continue placing the balls of stuffing along the edge without touching.

RECIPE CONTINUED ON NEXT PAGE

continued

CRABMEAT AGNOLOTTI

Yields 60 Agnolotti

RECIPE CONTINUED

When the line of stuffing is complete, take the edge of the dough closest to you and fold it over the enclose the stuffing. Carefully pinch the dough to encase the stuffing, expelling any air and encasing the stuffing completely. Fold over 1 more time. Use a pastry cutter to cut in between each mound of dough.

Line a baking pan with a sheet of parchment paper and dust with semolina.

Move the completed agnolotti to the pan. Repeat with the remaining dough and stuffing.

In a skillet over medium-high heat, bring the cream to a boil. Reduce the heat to a simmer and whisk in the butter. Continue whisking until the butter is incorporated. Remove from heat and whisk in the cheese until it is melted. Season with the sea salt and white pepper.

Bring a large pot of salted water to a boil. Cook the crab agnolotti in boiling salted water for 3 minutes. Remove and strain the agnolotti and add to the sauce.

CRAB QUESADILLA

Serves 8

1 pound jumbo lump crabmeat

sea salt to taste

fresh ground black pepper to taste

¼ cup green onions, sliced

2 tablespoons butter

2 ears of corn, cut off the cob

½ cup onion, peeled and diced

1 teaspoon garlic, minced

¼ cup cilantro, chopped

juice from 2 limes

16 small flour tortillas

1 pound grated Cheddar
(*or Monterey Jack*)

¼ cup vegetable oil

Cumin Lime Crema *(page 171)*

Place the crabmeat and green onions in a bowl and season, to taste, with salt and pepper. Set aside.

Melt the butter in a sauté pan over medium-high heat. Add the onions and sauté for 2 minutes. Add the corn and continue to cook for an additional 2 minutes. Stir in the garlic and season to taste with salt and pepper. Cook for 1 minute and remove from heat. Stir into the crab mixture and add the cilantro and lime juice. Taste for seasoning.

Place 8 tortillas on a table and spread ½ cup of the crabmeat mixture evenly over each tortilla. Place about a half cup of Cheddar cheese on top of the crabmeat. Cover each with a tortilla. Heat 2 tablespoons of the oil in a large griddle or non-stick skillet over medium heat. When hot, carefully lay the quesadilla in the oil. Fry on 1 side until golden brown, about 2 minutes, turn with a spatula and cook until golden brown on the second side and the cheese is melted, 1 to 2 minutes. Remove and repeat with the remaining quesadillas, adding more oil as needed.

To serve, cut each quesadilla into 4 triangles. Spread ¼ cup of the Cumin Lime Crema on each plate, and top with quesadilla quarters.

STUFFED CRAB BACKS

Serves 8 as Appetizer or 4 as Entrées

1 pound jumbo lump crabmeat

½ pound claw crabmeat

⅓ cup cracker meal

½ cup onion, peeled and chopped

1 teaspoon garlic, minced

4 green onions, sliced

¼ cup fresh Italian parsley, chopped

2 teaspoons fresh thyme, chopped

½ cup mayonnaise

1 egg, lightly beaten

1 teaspoon sea salt

½ teaspoon fresh ground black pepper

1 teaspoon Louisiana hot sauce

2 teaspoons Old Bay seasoning

1 teaspoon Worcestershire

1 teaspoon dry ground mustard

juice of 1 lemon

½ cup Panko bread crumbs

8 crab shells

8 pats of butter

Hollandaise sauce *(page 171)*

CHEF'S NOTES

After a boil, keep the backs of the crab to make a wonderful presentation for this dish. This recipe will also make a great stuffing for fish and other meats.

Preheat oven to 350° F.

In a mixing bowl, combine all of the ingredients except the pats of butter and mix well trying not to break up the lumps in the crab.

Stuff the crab shells with the crab stuffing, rounding the stuffing out of the top of the shells.

Place the crabs on a baking pan, top each crab with a pat of butter, and place the pan in the oven. Cook for 15 minutes until hot and bubbling.

Serve with Hollandaise sauce.

OYSTER SEASON

In the mid-1900s, my grandfather owned a local hardware store called "LaNasa Hardware" in the French Quarter. Oystermen would frequent the store to buy supplies for their boats and camps. Growing up, I remember the 50' oyster boat my grandfather built by hand in his own backyard. This was my first glimpse into the life of an oysterman, many of whom were Croatian.

Croatians are often considered the founders of the commercial oyster industry in Louisiana, dating from the 1800s. Many of today's current oystermen are 3rd and 4th generation Croatian families still delivering a great ingredient to our kitchens.

Oysters are one of those rare ingredients that can be just as delicious from the moment they are pulled onto the boat, cracked open and eaten raw, as when they're baked, grilled or fried. There is so much natural flavor in a Louisiana oyster. It's unlike any other oyster in the country and it's not by coincidence, either. Louisiana waters offer the perfect combination of fresh and saltwater. This is so important because the fresh water allows for incredible growth while the saltwater brings it delicious flavor. No other waters are able to produce such a large, flavorful oyster like Louisiana.

The cooler months are the perfect time for oysters. You've probably heard the saying "only eat oysters during months that have the letter 'r.'" While this is the time that Louisiana oysters are at their peak in size and flavor, it doesn't mean they can only be consumed during the cooler months. Louisiana produces delicious oysters that are safe to eat year-round; so don't worry, grab a sack and start shucking.

BACON BLOODY MARY SHOOTERS

Yields 24

6 slices bacon

2 cups Zing Zang Bloody Mary Mix

1 cup ketchup

1 tablespoon lemon juice

1 tablespoon lime juice

1 tablespoon prepared horseradish

1 tablespoon Worcestershire

1 teaspoon Louisiana hot sauce

sea salt to taste

fresh ground black pepper to taste

2 dozen shucked oysters

Creole seasoning *(page 166)*

cilantro sprigs

pickled okra

Render the bacon in a sauté pan over medium heat, turning as needed until the bacon is crisp. Remove the bacon and lay on a plate lined with paper towels. Reserve the bacon fat to cook with later. When cool, crumble the bacon.

In a small mixing bowl combine the crumbled bacon, Bloody Mary Mix, ketchup, lemon juice, lime juice, horseradish, Worcestershire, hot sauce, salt, and pepper.

Rub the rim of shot glasses with a lime wedge and dip in Creole seasoning to coat the rim. Place an oyster in the bottom of each shot glass and top with the Bloody Mary Mix.

Garnish with cilantro and sliced pickled okra.

Adding some of your favorite Vodka makes this a great adult hors d'oeuvres.

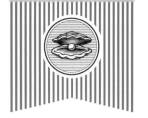

CHARBROILED OYSTERS

Serves 4

2 dozen fresh Gulf oysters

16 ounces butter

¼ cup tasso, diced

3 tablespoons garlic, diced

2 tablespoons shallots, diced

1 tablespoon fresh ground black pepper

1 tablespoon ground white pepper

1 tablespoon granulated garlic

1 cup grated Pecorino Romano cheese

1 cup grated Parmesan cheese

½ cup fresh Italian parsley, chopped

CHEF'S NOTES

Charbroiled oysters originated at Drago's Restaurant in Metairie, Louisiana, which is run by my good friend Tommy Cvitanovich and his family. The restaurant was founded by his father, Drago. The dish was actually created by dumb luck thanks to the menu item "Drumfish Tommy" at Drago's, which had a garlic butter baste. The story is told that one day, Tommy decided to try that same garlic butter on the oysters on the grill. Thus, Charbroiled Oysters were born. My recipe is a homage to the Drago's recipe. The main difference is the tasso which provides great smoke and spice flavors that pairs so well with the butter.

Preheat an outdoor grill to medium-high heat.

Make the garlic butter sauce by combining the butter, tasso, garlic, shallots, black pepper, white pepper, and granulated garlic, and set aside.

In a small bowl mix the cheeses.

Shuck the oysters and place a tablespoon of garlic butter sauce on each oyster. Place on the grill and allow to cook until the oyster plumps, about 7 minutes. Sprinkle with cheese and cook 1 more minute.

As the oysters cook, the butter will spill onto the grill and flare up. This is what gives the oysters their smoky character.

Sprinkle oysters with parsley and serve.

OYSTER & ARTICHOKE SOUP

Serves 12

1 pint oysters

1 cup butter

1 cup onion, peeled and chopped

½ cup leeks, white and light green parts only, sliced

½ cup fennel, bulb only, chopped

½ cup red bell pepper, seeded and chopped

¼ cup garlic, minced

½ cup tasso, chopped

2 - 10 ounce bags fresh spinach, chopped

1 cup flour

½ gallon chicken stock

1 pint heavy whipping cream

¼ cup green onions, sliced

¼ cup fresh Italian parsley, chopped

½ cup Herbsaint

sea salt to taste

fresh ground white pepper to taste

Tabasco to taste

CHEF'S NOTES

Oyster & Artichoke Soup was originally created by food chemist and restaurateur, Warren Leruth, at his famous restaurant Leruth's in Gretna, Louisiana, which closed in 1991. You've probably heard of him from his "Green Goddess Salad Dressing" fame. Warren Leruth passed away in 2001 and I serve this creamy bisque in memory of him and what he did for local cuisine.

In a heavy-bottomed stockpot, melt the butter over medium-high heat.

Add the onions, leeks, fennel, and bell pepper and sauté until softened, about 5 minutes. Add the garlic and tasso and cook for another minute. Add the spinach and chop it in the vegetable mixture with the spoon.

When it is well mixed, add the flour and stir to make a white roux. Do not let the roux brown. Cook it about 5 minutes.

Add any oyster water (from the oyster container) and the chicken stock while whisking and bring to a boil. Reduce heat to a simmer and cook about 20 minutes.

Add the heavy cream, green onions, parsley, and Herbsaint. Season to taste with salt and pepper. Add the oysters and cook until their edges begin to curl, about 1 minute.

SPINACH & OYSTER SALAD

Serves 4

½ pound applewood smoked bacon, diced

1 cup red onion, peeled and sliced

1 tablespoon garlic

¼ cup balsamic vinegar

2 tablespoons honey

¾ cup olive oil

1 teaspoon sea salt

½ teaspoon fresh ground black pepper

24 oysters, shucked

12 thin slices of bacon, halved

1 cup flour

½ cup masa harina

¼ cup corn meal

¼ cup corn starch

1 tablespoon Creole seasoning *(page 166)*

10 ounce bag of spinach

4 ounces fresh goat cheese

Render the bacon in a large sauté pan over medium-high heat. When the fat is rendered and the bacon is almost crisp, add the red onions and garlic and cook for 1 minute. Remove from heat and add the vinegar and honey and stir to combine. Pour into a mixing bowl and slowly stir in the olive oil while continuously whisking. Keep warm.

Preheat a fryer to 350° F. Wrap each oyster with a half slice of bacon. Secure with a toothpick. In a mixing bowl combine the flour, masa harina, corn meal, corn starch, and Creole seasoning and mix until well combined. Dredge the oysters in the corn batter, shaking off any excess. Add to the fryer and cook for about 3 minutes until the bacon is cooked. Remove from the fryer and drain on a plate lined with paper towels.

In a large mixing bowl, add the spinach and crumble in the goat cheese. Pour in the warm dressing and toss to coat.

Divide onto 4 plates and top with 6 bacon wrapped oysters.

OYSTER BIENVILLE

Serves 4

4 slices applewood smoked bacon, chopped

2 tablespoons butter

1 cup onion, peeled and chopped

1 tablespoon garlic, chopped

3 tablespoons flour

1 cup milk

½ cup brandy

⅔ cup mushrooms, chopped

½ pound shrimp, peeled and chopped

⅓ cup Parmesan cheese

1 tablespoon lemon juice

¼ cup green onions, sliced

¼ cup fresh Italian parsley, chopped

2 eggs, lightly beaten

¼ cup bread crumbs

sea salt to taste

fresh ground black pepper to taste

dash cayenne pepper, ground

dash Louisiana hot sauce

24 oysters, shucked and still in shell

Preheat the oven to 350° F.

In a large sauté pan over medium-high heat, render the bacon until crisp. Add the butter and the onion and stir until soft, about 5 minutes. Stir in the garlic and cook for 1 minute.

Stir in the flour to make a white roux. Cook for about 2 minutes (enough to cook out the flour taste but not enough to color).

Add the milk and brandy and whisk to remove any lumps. Add the mushrooms and shrimp and cook for 2 minutes. Turn off the heat and add the cheese, lemon juice, green onions, parsley, eggs, and bread crumbs. Season to taste with salt, pepper, and hot sauce.

Place 6 oysters in each of 4 small casserole dishes. Season with salt and pepper and cover with the Bienville sauce.

Bake about 12 minutes until hot and golden brown.

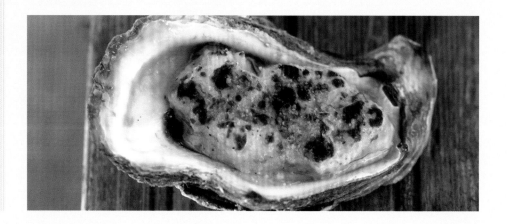

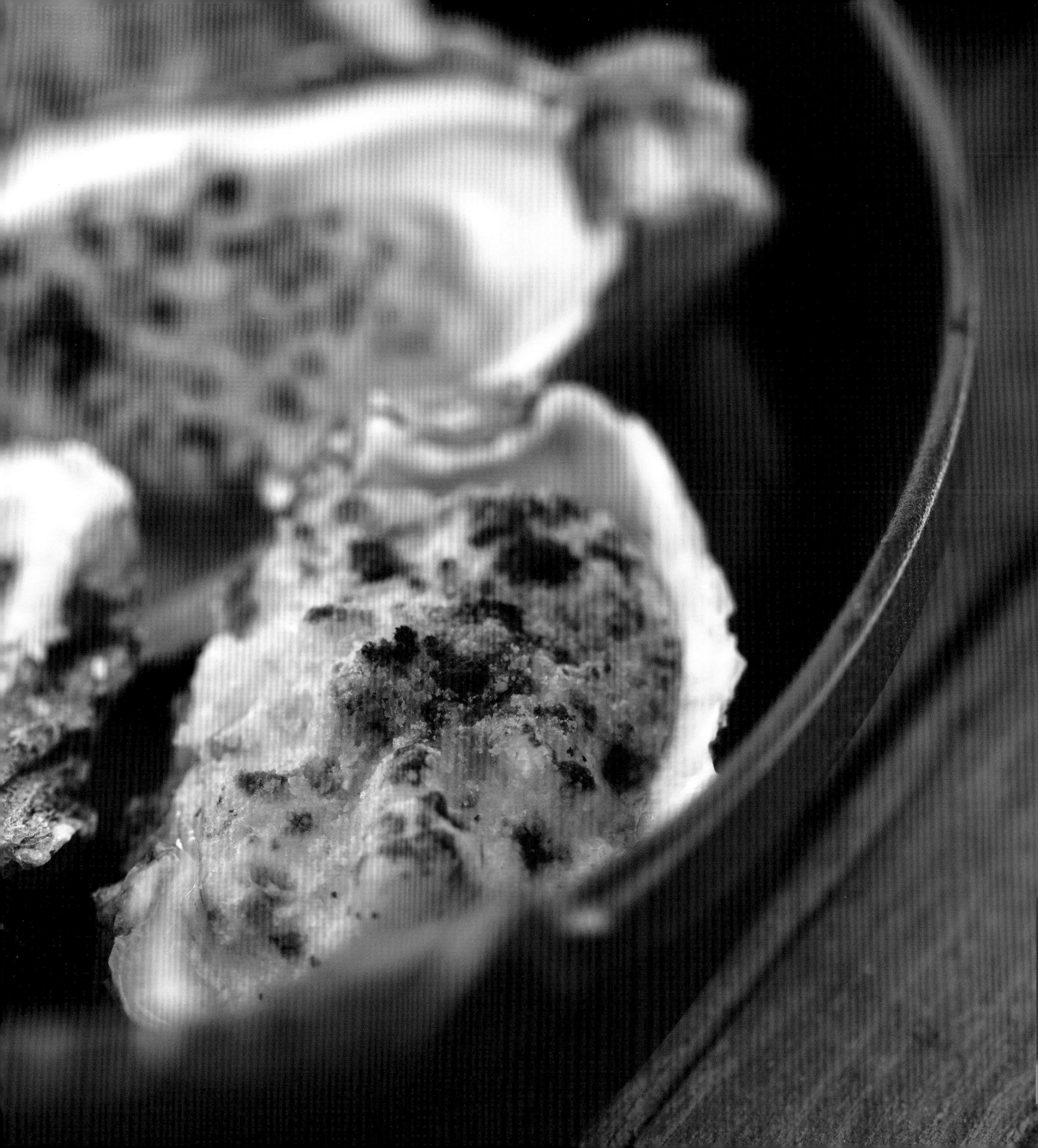

BUFFALO OYSTERS

Serves 6

½ cup Louisiana hot sauce

1 tablespoon garlic, chopped

¼ cup heavy whipping cream

1 stick of butter, cut into pieces

1 mirliton, peeled, seeded, and julienned

½ red onion, peeled and sliced

1 carrot, peeled and julienned

1 ounce Steen's cane vinegar

1 teaspoon sugar

1 teaspoon sea salt

1 teaspoon fresh ground black pepper

2 tablespoons cilantro, chopped

1 cup flour

½ cup masa harina

¼ cup corn starch

¼ cup corn meal

3 tablespoons Creole seasoning *(page 166)*, plus more for the oysters

freshly shucked oysters, approximately 6 dozen

CHEF'S NOTES

Buffalo wings were created in Buffalo, New York. Legend has it they were first created by the Anchor Bar in Buffalo, which is owned by Teressa Bellissimo and her husband, Frank. Some argue that it was another restaurant. While they disagree, we'll eat! The spice and butter works great with this southern rendition on fried oysters. If you want to add an even deeper southern twist, try our Bayou Wings on page 159.

In a small saucepan, combine the hot sauce with the garlic. Cook over medium heat until reduced by half. Stir in the cream and reduce for a couple of minutes more. Lower the heat and whisk in the butter a little at a time until it is emulsified. Strain and reserve in a warm spot.

In a large mixing bowl, combine the mirliton, red onions, and carrots. Blend in the vinegar, sugar, salt, pepper, and cilantro. Mix well and set aside.

Preheat a fryer to 350° F. In a large bowl whisk together the flour, masa harina, corn starch, corn meal, and Creole seasoning. Season the oysters with Creole seasoning and dust in the corn batter. Lower into the hot oil and fry for about 2 minutes until crisp. Remove from the oil and place on a plate lined with several layers of paper towels.

Place some slaw in the center of a plate. Toss the oysters in the sauce and place them around the slaw. Serve more sauce on the side.

OYSTER VONGOLE

Serves 4

1 pound spaghetti

2 tablespoons olive oil

½ cup onion, peeled and chopped

1 tablespoon garlic, minced

½ teaspoon red pepper flakes

½ cup white wine

2 cups heavy whipping cream

1 teaspoon oregano

1 bay leaf

2 tablespoons fresh Italian parsley, chopped

2 tablespoons green onions, sliced

sea salt to taste

fresh ground black pepper to taste

48 freshly shucked oysters

½ cup Pecorino Romano cheese

CHEF'S NOTES

This is a classic recipe from my grandfather's restaurant. Vongole is the Italian word for clams. Here we take a traditional Italian dish made with clams and substitute oysters.

Bring a large pot of salted water to a boil. The water should taste like the sea. When it is rapidly boiling, add the spaghetti and stir to separate the pasta. Cook until the pasta is al dente, cooked through but still firm to the bite. Drain.

Meanwhile, heat the olive oil in a large sauté pan over medium-high heat. Add the onions and cook for 2 minutes until soft. Add the garlic and crushed red pepper and stir for 1 minute. Deglaze with white wine and cook until reduced by half.

Add the cream, oregano, and bay leaf and bring to a boil. Cook for 2 minutes longer then add the oysters, parsley, and green onions. Cook until the edges of the oysters begin to curl then season with salt and pepper.

Toss with the cheese and hot spaghetti.

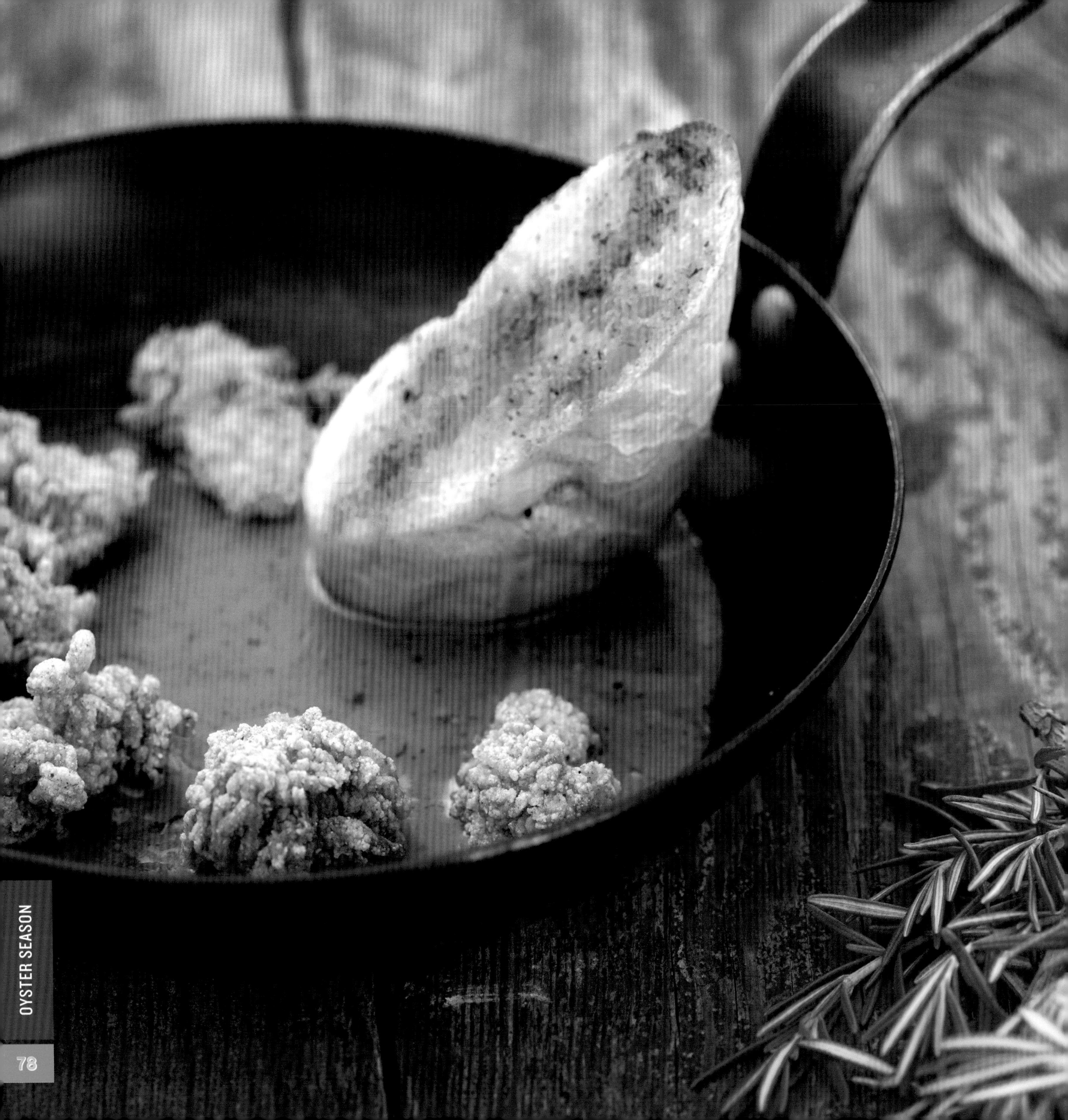

New Orleans Style

BBQ OYSTERS

⊢ *Serves 4* ⊣

1 pound butter, cut into chips,
at room temperature

1 tablespoon fresh ground black pepper

2 tablespoons Creole seasoning *(page 166)*

3 tablespoons Worcestershire sauce

2 tablespoons garlic, chopped

juice of 1 ½ lemons

2 tablespoons fresh rosemary, minced

2 tablespoons fresh Italian parsley, chopped

2 tablespoons green onions, sliced

2 tablespoons olive oil

4 ounces Budweiser beer

4 dozen oysters, shucked

To make the barbecue butter, place the butter, black pepper, Creole seasoning, Worcestershire, garlic, lemon juice, rosemary, parsley, and green onions in a food processor. Blend until completely smooth and well blended.

Heat the beer in a sauté pan over medium-high heat.

Add the oysters and cook until the oysters begin to plump. Lower the heat to a simmer and whisk in the butter 1 tablespoon at a time until it is creamy and you have used about half of the butter.

Divide into 4 four bowls and serve hot with warm French bread.

CREOLE TOMATO SEASON

On the Eastbank of New Orleans lives a man named Mr. Gallo. I still call him "Mister" since I've known him since I was a child. He sold tomatoes to my grandfather and father, and now he sells to me. For three generations I have gone to only one place for Creole tomatoes: Mr. Gallo's farm. One of my earliest memories with my grandfather is walking through a tomato garden. He would pull a tomato right off the vine, whip out a pocket knife and salt shaker and share a fresh tomato right there with me.

As an Italian living in the south, it just doesn't get any better than Creole tomato season. Every trip I make to Mr. Gallo's farm takes me back to my childhood. The season lasts for a few weeks beginning in early summer, depending on the rain and heat. Farmers traditionally plant their seeds — which are passed on from generation to generation — on Good Friday.

Creole tomatoes are allowed to ripen on the vine before being picked, unlike other tomatoes that are picked green, then gassed to become ripe. Creole tomatoes are grown south of New Orleans on either side of the Mississippi River. The crops benefit from the alluvial soils that came after the frequent flooding of the levees. This made for incredible soil to plant seeds after the levees were built to withstand the flooding.

As you begin cooking the best produce New Orleans has to offer, keep this tip in mind: When you bring your fresh produce home from the market, never put it by the bananas. Bananas release a gas that causes other produce to over-ripen and spoil. I've never liked bananas, even as a kid. I now know why! Not only do I hate the taste, but they can ruin my beloved Creole tomatoes!

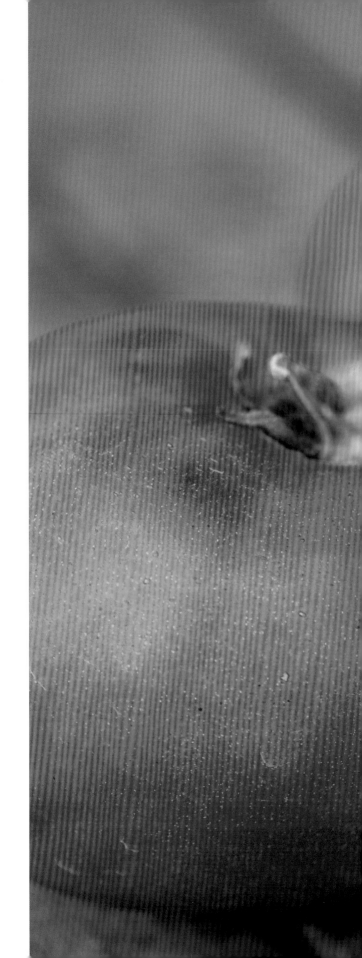

CREOLE TOMATO

TOMATO, WATERMELON, & FETA SALAD

Serves 4

2 cups watermelon, rind and seeds removed,
cut into 1" cubes

2 cups Creole tomatoes, core removed,
cut into 1" cubes

6 cups wild arugula, washed

1 cup Feta cheese, crumbled

½ cup red onion, peeled and chopped

½ cup pine nuts, toasted

1 cup olive oil

½ cup balsamic glaze

sea salt to taste

fresh ground black pepper to taste

In a large mixing bowl, combine the watermelon, tomatoes, arugula, Feta, red onion, and pine nuts.

Toss to mix, then add the olive oil, balsamic glaze, salt and pepper.

Toss again and divide evenly among 4 plates.

CRISPY CREOLE TOMATO

with Crab Ravigote

Serves 4 large or 8 small portions

8 ½" slices from a firm Creole tomato

sea salt to taste

fresh ground black pepper to taste

1 cup flour

2 tablespoons Creole seasoning *(page 166)*

1 cup milk

1 egg

1 cup plain bread crumbs

¼ cup Romano cheese, grated

1 teaspoon oregano, dried

1 tablespoon fresh Italian parsley, chopped

1 teaspoon granulated onion

1 ½ teaspoons granulated garlic

1 recipe Crabmeat Ravigote *(page 45)*

½ cup petite or micro herbs
(parsley or chervil can be substituted)

CHEF'S NOTES

Here is my version of a fried green tomato. When selecting a Creole tomato for this recipe, choose a very firm tomato so it won't break apart when frying. You could also top this dish with shrimp and remoulade sauce from the Sclafani Salad recipe on page 13.

Preheat the fryer to 350° F.

Season each side of the tomato slices with salt and pepper. In a small bowl, combine the flour and 1 tablespoon of Creole seasoning and mix well. In another small bowl, combine the milk and egg and beat until well combined. In another small bowl, mix the bread crumbs, Romano cheese, oregano, parsley, granulated onion, and granulated garlic until well combined.

Take a couple of slices of tomato and dust in the flour, shaking off any excess. Dip into the egg wash submerging the tomato slices completely. Remove, shaking off any excess. Dust in the Italian bread crumbs making sure the tomato is completely coated.

Shake off any excess and lay in the preheated fryer. Cook for about 2 minutes or until the tomato is crispy and golden brown. Remove from the fryer and set aside on paper towels to drain.

Repeat with the remaining tomato slices. Divide the tomatoes on the plates and top each tomato with 2 to 3 tablespoons of crab ravigote. Garnish with micro or petite herbs.

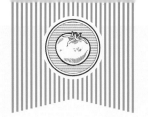

CREOLE TOMATO SOUP

with Crab & Brie Panini

⊣ *Serves 12* ⊢

For the Creole Tomato Soup:

2 tablespoons olive oil

1 cup onion, peeled and chopped

1 tablespoon garlic, minced

8 cups Creole tomatoes, peeled, seeded, and diced
(*or crushed San Marzano tomatoes*)

2 cups chicken stock

1 teaspoon fresh thyme, chopped

1 teaspoon oregano, dried

1 bay leaf

1 tablespoon sugar

2 teaspoons sea salt

1 teaspoon fresh ground black pepper

½ teaspoon cayenne pepper, ground

¼ cup basil, chiffonade

1 cup heavy whipping cream

For the Crab & Brie Panini:

1 loaf French bread, New Orleans style

1 cup salted butter, melted

1 pound jumbo lump crabmeat

1 bunch green onions, sliced

sea salt to taste

fresh ground black pepper to taste

1 pound Brie, rind removed

For the Creole Tomato Soup:

In a large stockpot, heat the oil over medium-high heat. Add the onions and cook for 5 minutes until soft. Add the garlic and cook for 1 more minute. Stir in the tomatoes and chicken stock and bring to a boil. Reduce the heat to a simmer and stir in the thyme, oregano, bay leaf, sugar, salt, and peppers. Simmer for 20 minutes. Remove from heat and remove the bay leaf. Purée using an immersion blender. Allow to cool first if using a regular blender. Return to a simmer and stir in the heavy cream and basil. Taste for seasoning.

For the Crab & Brie Panini:

Slice the bread into ¼" thick slices. Lightly brush each side of the bread with butter and set aside.

In a small mixing bowl, add the crabmeat, green onions, salt, and pepper, and mix well. Cut the Brie into small slices to fit on the French bread, no longer than 2".

Place a tablespoon of crabmeat on a piece of buttered bread, top with a slice of Brie and place another slice of buttered bread on top. Press down slightly.

Heat a non-stick sauté pan over medium heat. Put down a layer of crab sandwiches, but do not crowd the pan. Cook for a couple of minutes until the bread is golden brown. Carefully flip the sandwiches and brown on the other side. This gentle heat should melt the cheese and heat the crabmeat through. Repeat until all of the sandwiches are done.

CREOLE TOMATO SALAD

with Burrata & Balsamic Caviar

⊢ *Serves 4* ⊣

For the Balsamic Caviar:

200 grams balsamic vinegar

1.6 grams Agar Agar

2 quarts vegetable oil, very cold,
in a tall, thin container

For the Salad:

3 heirloom tomatoes in
preferably different varieties

sea salt and fresh ground black pepper

8 ounces Burrata cheese
(Mozzarella can be substituted)

½ cup balsamic caviar
(balsamic vinegar can be substituted)

micro basil
(regular basil can be substituted)

extra virgin olive oil

CHEF'S NOTES

This is one of my favorite dishes. It won a Gold Fleur De Lis Culinary Award at the New Orleans Wine and Food Experience and I served it at a special dinner I prepared at the James Beard House in New York City, which is a highlight of my culinary career. This is my modern version of a traditional caprese salad. Instead of Mozzarella, I use Burrata cheese, which is Italian for "butter." I also use a molecular gastronomy technique to create spheres of balsamic vinegar. Download the free "Ruffino's at Home" iPad app to see this unusual technique in action.

Using a blender or immersion blender, blend the balsamic creating a vortex. Slowly add the agar agar into the vortex to hydrate. Pour the vinegar into a sauce pot and bring to a simmer over medium heat. Allow to simmer for 1 minute then remove from heat. Allow the vinegar to cool to about 120° F. Place the container with the cold vegetable oil in an ice bath to keep the oil cold. Pour the vinegar into a squeeze bottle and drop into the cold oil. Keep the squeeze bottle moving so the droplets do not touch each other until they hit the bottom of the container. The vinegar must cool to below 80° F before hitting the bottom of the container. If the vinegar in the squeeze bottle gets too cool and starts to solidify, reheat slowly and drop into the cold oil again. When all of the vinegar has been spherified, drain the oil through a fine sieve, saving the oil and the "caviar" separately. Store extra caviar in a covered container in the refrigerator.

Slice the heirloom tomatoes into ⅓" thick slices and arrange 3 different colored slices on each plate. Season the tomatoes with sea salt and fresh ground black pepper. Place a heaping tablespoon of Burrata cheese on top of each tomato, trying to get some of the rind and some of the softer cheese together. Place a teaspoon of balsamic caviar on each piece of Burrata. Arrange micro basil on each slice of tomato and drizzle with extra virgin olive oil.

PANEE VEAL VINAIGRETTE

Serves 4

For the Vinaigrette:

1 cup ripe Creole tomatoes, cut into wedges

1 cup Vidalia onions, peeled and sliced
(can substitute other sweet onions)

½ cup lemon juice

1 teaspoon dried oregano

1 tablespoon fresh Italian parsley, chopped

1 tablespoon garlic, chopped

2 teaspoons sea salt

½ teaspoon fresh ground black pepper

4 ice cubes

1 ½ cups extra virgin olive oil

For the Veal:

12 (2 ounces) veal medallions, cut from the leg

3 tablespoons Creole seasoning *(page 166)*

1 cup flour

1 cup milk

1 egg

1 cup plain bread crumbs

¼ cup Romano cheese, grated

1 teaspoon dried oregano

1 tablespoon fresh Italian parsley, chopped

1 teaspoon granulated onion

1 ½ teaspoons granulated garlic

olive oil

CHEF'S NOTES

Panee is a term we used in New Orleans for something that is lightly breaded and fried. We pair the veal with a light vinaigrette to offset the richness of the fried veal.

In a large mixing bowl, combine the tomato wedges, onions, lemon juice, oregano, parsley, garlic, salt, pepper, and ice cubes. While stirring with a large spoon, slowly add in the olive oil. Set aside.

Place one slice of veal in a heavy gallon sized zip-lock bag. Flatten and spread the veal with a meat mallet. Remove from the bag and lightly season with Creole seasoning on both sides and set aside. Repeat with the remaining pieces of veal.

In a small bowl, combine the flour and 1 tablespoon of Creole seasoning and mix well. In another small bowl, combine the milk and egg and beat until well combined. In another small bowl, mix the bread crumbs, Romano cheese, oregano, parsley, granulated onion, and granulated garlic until well combined.

Dredge each slice of veal in the seasoned flour shaking off any excess. Dip each slice in the egg wash shaking off the excess then dip in the seasoned bread crumbs. Set aside.

Heat a sauté pan over medium-high heat and add olive oil to coat the bottom of the pan. When the oil is hot, add the veal slices a few pieces at a time, not crowding the pan. Cook for about 2 minutes and then flip and cook for 2 more minutes. The veal should be golden brown. Remove to a plate covered with paper towels. Repeat with the remaining veal slices. Place 3 slices of veal on each plate. Mix the sauce well and ladle some of the tomatoes and onions on the veal along with some of the sauce.

CAPELLINI GAMBERI

Serves 6

1 pound angel hair pasta

sea salt

2 tablespoons olive oil

3 pounds large shrimp, peeled and deveined

3 tablespoons Creole seasoning *(page 166)*

1 ½ tablespoons garlic, chopped

3 cups Creole tomatoes, peeled, seeded, and diced

⅓ cup lemon juice

½ cup basil, chiffonade

sea salt to taste

fresh ground black pepper to taste

1 ½ tablespoons white truffle oil *(optional)*

Bring a large pot of water to a rolling boil. Season the water with sea salt until it tastes like the ocean. Add the angel hair pasta and stir well. Cook at a rolling boil until the pasta is al dente (firm but not crunchy), about 4 minutes.

Drain the pasta.

Meanwhile, heat a large sauté pan over medium-high heat. While the sauté pan is heating, season the shrimp with the Creole seasoning.

Add the oil to the pan and when it shimmers add the shrimp and toss so they do not stick to the bottom of the pan. Cook for 1 minute the add the garlic and stir.

Add the Creole tomatoes and lemon juice and stir. Cook for another minute and add the basil and cooked angel hair. Toss until well distributed.

Divide evenly among 6 bowls. Drizzle in the truffle oil, if using.

FISHING SEASON

Growing up in Louisiana, my weekends were consumed with what you might expect: hunting and fishing. I remember fishing practically every weekend with brother Gino and my Dad. We would fish throughout south Louisiana. Lake Pontchartrain, Bayou Bienvenue, Delacroix, Shell Beach and Grand Isle were our favorites. During that time, the fishing limits weren't as minimal as today and you could even sell your own fish at the restaurant for dinner. Nothing brought being a chef full circle like serving guests the very fish you caught that morning. It couldn't get any fresher!

Our catch was primarily saltwater, consisting of speckled trout, redfish and flounder. The seasons and weather would primarily dictate our fishing.

In the winter, we would explore the shallow flats since the fish would be dormant; and we'd tackle the deeper waters in the summer.

The best part of fishing, of course, is the stories. You have yours and, well, we definitely have ours! Nothing beats an early morning of fishing followed by a great evening swapping stories while cooking the fresh catch. In the following pages, you'll find my favorite recipes to prepare after a day on the boat. This chapter features some of the most versatile recipes because you can substitute just about any catch as you see fit.

FISHING

AHI TUNA TARTARE

Serves 6

1 pound fresh ahi tuna, small dice

½ cup cucumber, peeled, seeded and diced

1 tablespoon jalapeño, seeded and minced

¼ cup green onions, thinly sliced

2 tablespoons soy sauce

1 teaspoon Sriracha

1 teaspoon sesame oil

juice of ½ a lime

2 avocados, peeled, seeded, and diced

juice of ½ a lime

1 cup micro greens or herb mix
(cilantro, Italian parsley, chervil, chives)

10 egg roll wrappers

cooking oil for deep frying

1 teaspoon Chinese 5 spice powder

1 cup mayonnaise

1 ½ tablespoons Sriracha

¾ tablespoons soy sauce

1 teaspoon sesame oil

1 teaspoon sesame seeds

Preheat the fryer to 350° F. In a small mixing bowl, combine the tuna, cucumber, jalapeño, green onions, soy sauce, Sriracha, sesame oil, and lime juice. Mix well and refrigerate.

In a small mixing bowl toss the avocado with the lime juice. Mix well and refrigerate.

Cut the egg roll wrappers in half on a diagonal from corner to corner and then in half again from the other corner to make 4 small triangles. Carefully separate and drop in the hot oil a few at a time. Fry for about 1 minute or until crisp. Drain and place on a plate lined with paper towels. Dust with some of the Chinese 5 spice powder.

In another small mixing bowl, combine the mayonnaise, Sriracha, soy sauce, and sesame oil, and whisk to incorporate.

Place a 3" ring mold on one side of a plate. Fill ¾ of the way with the tuna mixture. Fill the remainder with diced avocado. Top with a quarter of the micro greens or herb mix. Remove the ring mold and drizzle the sauce on the opposite side of the plate. Repeat 3 more times and garnish with a sprinkling of sesame seeds. Serve with won ton chips.

As an alternative, place some of the spicy mayo on each of the won ton chips. Spoon on some of the chilled tuna tartare and diced avocado and garnish with sesame seeds.

REDFISH BEIGNETS

⊢ *Yields 36 Beignets* ⊣

2 large eggs

1 pound redfish fillets, diced (about 2 cups)

1 tablespoon Creole seasoning *(page 166)*

¼ cup red bell peppers, seeded and diced

¼ cup green onions, sliced

1 tablespoon garlic, minced

1 teaspoon fresh thyme, chopped

2 teaspoon fresh lemon zest

1 teaspoon fine sea salt

½ teaspoon fresh ground black pepper

1 ½ cups all-purpose flour

1 teaspoon baking powder

½ cup Abita™ Amber beer

2 tablespoons Creole seasoning *(page 166)*

Creole remoulade sauce *(page 171)*

Preheat the fryer to 350° F.

In a large bowl whisk the eggs until frothy. Add the crawfish to the eggs and season with Creole seasoning. Stir in the bell peppers, green onions, garlic, salt, flour, baking powder, and milk, and stir until it has the consistency of wet dough. Makes about 2 cups.

When the oil is hot, drop in about half the beignet mixture by large spoonfuls and fry until golden brown and crispy, for about 3 minutes *(do this in batches to avoid overcrowding)*. Drain the beignets on paper towels.

Serve with Creole remoulade sauce for dipping.

Sclafani's
RED SNAPPER SOUP

⊢ *Serves 12* ⊢

¼ cup olive oil

1 cup onion, peeled and diced

1 cup leeks, white and light green parts, chopped

1 cup fennel, bulb only, diced

½ cup green bell pepper, seeded and diced

1 tablespoon garlic, chopped

1 tablespoon oregano, whole dry leaves

1 tablespoon fresh thyme, chopped

4 bay leaves, whole dry leaves

5 tablespoons flour

2 quarts fish stock *(page 167)*

2 cups canned San Marzano tomatoes, squeezed

1 tablespoon sea salt

2 teaspoons fresh ground black pepper

½ teaspoon crushed red pepper

2 red snapper fillets, cut into small dices
(about 3 cups)

1 tablespoon fresh Italian parsley, chopped

2 tablespoons green onion, sliced thin

CHEF'S NOTES

This is another recipe from my grandfather's Restaurant Sclafani on Causeway Boulevard in New Orleans. We wanted to utilize the entire fish in the restaurant, and the perfect way to do that after it was filleted was to make a good fish stock. That's the basis of this recipe. You can substitute your fresh catch for snapper to personalize this dish.

Heat the olive oil in a heavy bottomed stockpot over medium-high heat.

Add the onions and cook for 2 minutes. Add the fennel and bell pepper and cook for 2 minutes. Add the garlic, oregano, thyme, and bay leaves and stir for 1 minute more.

Stir in the flour and cook while stirring for 2 minutes. Do not let the flour brown. Add the stock, while stirring, a little at a time. Add the tomatoes and their juice and the salt and peppers. Bring to a boil and reduce the heat to a simmer. Simmer for 10 minutes.

Add the red fish pieces, parsley, and green onions and continue to simmer for 5 more minutes.

Adjust the seasoning to taste.

TUNA NICOISE SALAD

Serves 4

4 (4 ounce) pieces of fresh yellowfin tuna

sea salt to taste

fresh ground black pepper to taste

¼ cup olive oil

6 cups spring mix or baby arugula

Nicoise Salad Dressing *(page 166)*

1 ½ cups haricots vert, blanched and chilled *(baby French green beans)*,

12 red potatoes, boiled, chilled, and quartered

½ pint cherry or grape tomatoes, halved

¾ cup black olives, pitted and halved *(I prefer Nicoise, Kalamata, or oil cured)*

½ red onion, peeled and sliced thin

4 hard boiled eggs, peeled and quartered

CHEF'S NOTES

This dish is a classic French salad from the Nice region in France. Instead of using canned tuna as the traditional recipe does, I use freshly seared tuna.

Heat a skillet over medium-high heat. Season the tuna with salt and pepper, pressing it into the fish. Add the oil to the skillet and when it begins to smoke, add the tuna. Do not crowd the pan. Cook in batches if necessary. Cook approximately 2 minutes on each side until golden on the outside but still rare in the middle. Adjust time based on the thickness of the tuna. Remove to a plate and set aside to rest.

In a large mixing bowl, toss the lettuce with enough dressing just to coat the leaves. Divide onto 4 plates. In the same mixing bowl, add the haricots vert, potatoes, tomatoes, olives, and red onions, and toss with enough dressing to coat. Divide even among the four plates.

Slice the tuna into thin slices. Fan the tuna over each of the salads. Arrange the quartered eggs on each plate.

SPECKLED TROUT POMODORO

Serves 8

1 pint cherry tomatoes, quartered

4 sun-dried tomatoes, chopped

1 teaspoon garlic, chopped

2 tablespoons green onions, sliced

1 tablespoon fresh Italian parsley, chopped

12 basil leaves, chiffonade

½ teaspoon dried oregano

1 teaspoon sea salt

½ teaspoon fresh ground black pepper

¼ cup extra virgin olive oil

8 (8 ounce) fillets of speckled trout
(red snapper, redfish, pompano, drum, etc. may be substituted)

8 sheets of parchment paper, 12"x20", folded in half, cut into a large heart

2 tablespoons Creole seasoning *(page 166)*

CHEF'S NOTES

The dish was originally crafted for a French balloonist who was being entertained at Antoine's Restaurant in New Orleans. The paper bag was fashioned to resemble an inflated balloon. However, its real purpose was to retain the wonderful flavors of the fish and seasonings. This recipe works great with any flaky white fish and offers a healthy option with easy cleanup.

For the Marinated Tomatoes:

Combine the cherry tomatoes, sun dried tomatoes, garlic, green onion, parsley, basil, oregano, salt, pepper, and olive oil in a large stainless bowl and let it marinate for 2 hours.

For the Fish:

Place ¼ cup of marinated tomatoes and juices on one half of the parchment. Season the fish on both sides with Creole seasoning and place presentation side (side closest to the bone, not the skin side) down on top of the tomatoes.

Fold the parchment in half over the fish. Beginning at the seam, make a small fold and press the crease. Make the next fold by folding the previous fold in half. Continue along the edges creating a continuous seam. When you get to the end, fold the last piece under the fish. Turn the fish over so the presentation side is facing up.

Bake in a preheated oven at 400° F for 12 to 15 minutes. The parchment bag should be puffed up and beginning to brown slightly.

Serve immediately and cut open at the table to release the amazing aroma in front of your guests.

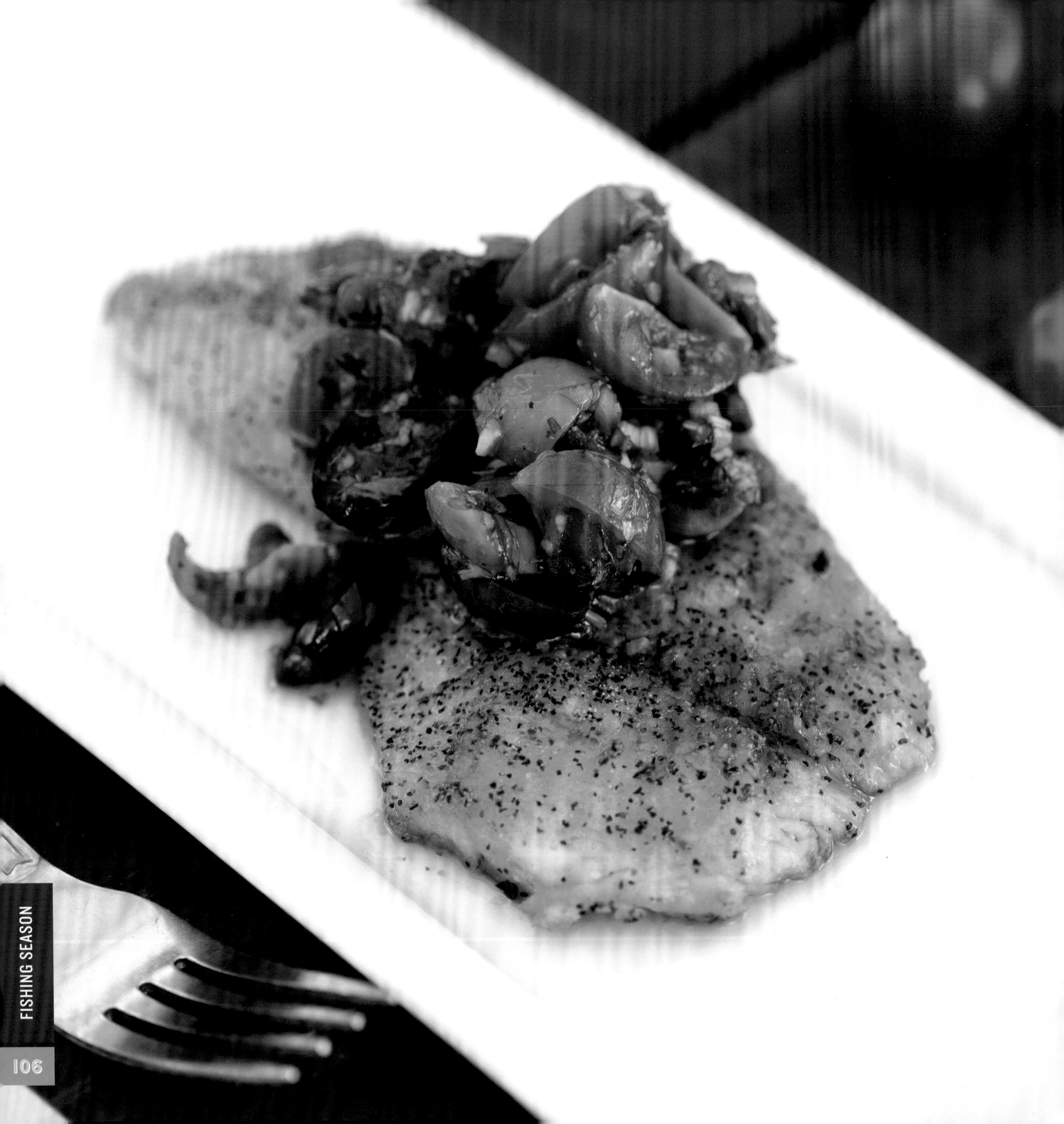

SICILIAN STYLE TRIPLE TAIL

Serves 4

¼ cup extra virgin olive oil

½ cup red onion, peeled and finely chopped

2 tablespoons garlic, chopped

1 pint cherry tomatoes, cut in ¼

⅔ cup black olives, pitted and halved
(nicoise, kalamata, or oil cured)

⅔ cup green olives, pitted and halved

4 anchovies, finely chopped

2 tablespoons fresh Italian parsley, chopped

2 tablespoons green onions, sliced

2 tablespoons fresh basil, chiffonade

1 teaspoon dried oregano

2 teaspoons sea salt

½ teaspoon fresh ground black pepper

2 tablespoons capers

2 ounces balsamic vinegar

4 (6 ounce) fillets of Tripletail
(almost any kind of fish may be substituted)

1 tablespoon Creole seasoning *(page 166)*

2 tablespoons olive oil

2 tablespoons butter

Combine olive oil, red onion, garlic, tomatoes, olives, anchovies, parsley, basil, green onions, oregano, salt and pepper, capers, and balsamic vinegar in a large mixing bowl and mix well. Allow to sit at room temperature for 1 hour before serving.

Preheat an oven to 350° F.

Season the fish on both sides with Creole seasoning.

Heat the olive oil and butter in a large sauté pan over medium-high heat.

When hot, place the fish presentation side down (side that is closest to the bone, not the skin side). Cook for 3-4 minutes until the fish is golden brown. Carefully flip the fish and place the sauté pan in the oven.

Allow to cook in the oven approximately 6-8 minutes or until the fish is just cooked through. Time will depend on the thickness and density of each type of fish.

Place a fillet of fish on each of 4 plates. Top with some of the tomato and olive sauce.

FISHING

TUNA PUTTANESCA

with Penne

Serves 6

1 pound penne pasta (or pasta of your choice)

¼ cup olive oil

1 cup red onion, peeled and chopped

1 tablespoon garlic, chopped

8 each anchovy, chopped

28 ounce can San Marzano tomatoes, crushed by hand with juice

1 cup black olives, pitted and halved *(nicoise, kalamata, or oil cured)*

½ cup capers

½ teaspoon crushed red pepper flakes

1 teaspoon dried oregano

2 pounds fresh yellowfin tuna, cut into ½" cubes

½ cup fresh basil, torn into small pieces

¼ cup green onions, sliced

2 tablespoons fresh Italian parsley, chopped

sea salt to taste

fresh ground black pepper to taste

CHEF'S NOTES

This is an incredibly versatile and easy dish that can quickly feed your entire family on a busy weeknight. You can even experiment with your favorite meat or seafood. You can't go wrong. The aroma alone will draw everyone to the table!

Bring a large pot of salted water to a rolling boil. The water should taste like the ocean. Add the pasta and stir. Cook until the pasta is al dente, tender but still firm to the bite. Drain.

Meanwhile, heat the olive oil in a large dutch oven over medium-high heat. Add the onions and cook for 2 minutes. Add the garlic and anchovy and stir for 1 minute. Pour in the tomatoes and bring to a boil. Reduce the heat to a simmer and add the olives, capers, crushed red pepper, and oregano. Simmer for 5 minutes. Add the tuna, basil, green onions, and parsley. Cook the tuna for about 2 minutes. Taste and adjust seasoning with sea salt and pepper. Add the pasta and stir until well combined.

Divide into 6 pasta bowls. Serve hot.

HOLIDAY SEASON

I have to be honest, as a Chef the holidays to me mean the busiest time for the restaurant. From Thanksgiving to Christmas are the longest hour days without a single day off. The work is hard, but we know that it's for a special reason.

Everyone is traveling to gather with their family and it's a fitting time to wind down the year. You probably think that with a family of Chefs our Thanksgiving and Christmas meals were something off the cover of a Food & Wine magazine. I'll admit, the food is good but what I remember most about the dinner isn't the meal itself but the prepping and sourcing all the ingredients.

When you have lots of family coming in a good plan is a necessity. It's easy to get caught up in the hustle of the holidays but some of the best memories I feel you will ever create are in that gray area when things don't go as planned. You'll always remember that time someone almost caught the house on fire or something was forgotten, those moments are the stories that continue to tell themselves over and over throughout the years.

Even though we were working long hours during these times, the memories are still there. The trips I would take with my father the days before Christmas to make sure we have everything we needed before the big day were some great memories. It's in those trips we would take to see the local suppliers and learn about their stories in Louisiana that I found my passion. We weren't just serving food, we were serving food that had a story which has become my driving philosophy in the kitchen.

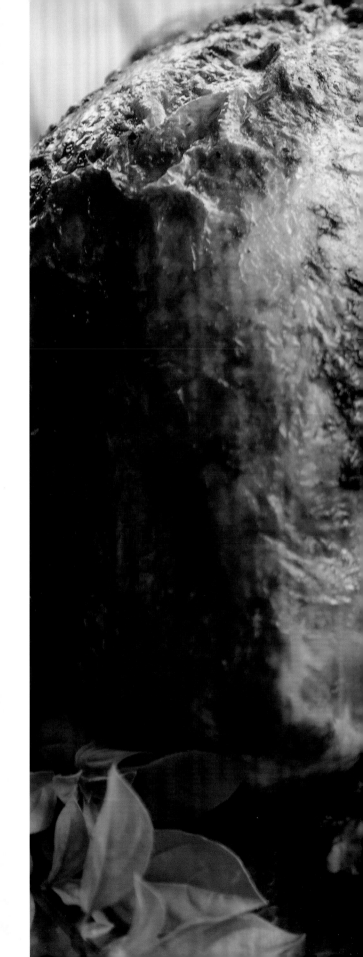

BUTTERNUT SQUASH RAVIOLI
with Sage Browned Butter
Serves 6

1 large butternut squash, about 2 pounds

¼ cup olive oil

sea salt to taste

fresh ground black pepper to taste

½ cup + ½ cup Parmigiano-Reggiano cheese, grated

2 tablespoons butter

1 pasta dough recipe

semolina flour for dusting

2 sticks butter

12 sage leaves

Preheat an oven to 350° F.

Cut the squash in half lengthwise and remove the seeds and membranes with a spoon. Rub the cut side on the squash with the olive oil and place cut side down on a sheet pan.

Bake for 1 hour or until the squash can be pierced easily with a knife. Remove from the oven and allow to cool slightly.

Scrape the flesh of the squash into a food processor. Season the squash with sea salt and pepper. Add ½ cup of the cheese and purée. Add the butter and purée again.

To make the ravioli, cut the dough into 4 pieces. Remove one piece and wrap the remaining pieces. Flatten the dough and dust it with semolina. Set the pasta machine to position 1. Pass the dough through, fold it in half and dust with semolina. Repeat this process about 7 or 8 times. The dough should not be sticky and should feel silky.

Now turn the setting to 2 and pass through. Repeat, increasing the setting by one each time until you get to position 5. Dust the dough in semolina and run it through position 5 three times. Lay the dough on a lightly floured surface. Place 1 tablespoon of the stuffing in the center of the dough starting 1" from the edge. Place another tablespoon of stuffing every 2".

Roll out another sheet of pasta as above and lay over the sheet with the stuffing.

Carefully press down on the top sheet around the filling, expelling any air. Using a ravioli cutter or fluted pastry wheel, cut in between the mounds of stuffing into individual raviolis.

RECIPE CONTINUED ON NEXT PAGE ▶

BUTTERNUT SQUASH RAVIOLI

with Sage Browned Butter

⊢ *Serves 6* ⊣

RECIPE CONTINUED

Line a baking pan with a sheet of parchment paper and dust with semolina. Move the completed ravioli to the pan. Repeat with the remaining dough and stuffing.

Bring a large pot of salted water to a boil. The water should taste like the ocean. Add the ravioli and stir gently. Cook for 4 minutes.

Meanwhile, in a large sauté pan, heat the butter over medium-high heat.

Cook until the butter has stopped foaming and turns a nutty brown color. Add the sage leaves and immediately add the drained ravioli. Toss gently to coat and divide onto 6 plates.

Garnish with the remaining cheese.

TURKEY, OYSTER, & ANDOUILLE GUMBO

Serves 16-20

1 turkey, 8 - 10 pounds, with giblets

1 onion, peeled and sliced

2 ribs celery, sliced

1 carrot, peeled and sliced

5 cloves of garlic, smashed

4 bay leaves

2 tablespoons black peppercorns

1 tablespoon coriander seeds

1 bunch fresh thyme

1 bunch parsley stems

1 cup vegetable oil

1 ½ cups flour

2 cups onions, peeled and chopped

1 cup celery, chopped

1 green bell pepper, seeded and chopped

1 tablespoon garlic, chopped

2 bay leaves

2 cups andouille, halved lengthwise then sliced

2 tablespoons fresh thyme, chopped

1 pint oysters, with liquid

sea salt and fresh ground black pepper to taste

Louisiana hot sauce to taste

¼ cup fresh Italian parsley, chopped

½ cup green onions, sliced

2 tablespoons + 2 tablespoons filé, ground

½ gallon cooked white rice

In a stockpot, place the turkey with giblets, onions, celery, carrot, and garlic and cover with cold water, about 2 gallons. Cut a 8"x8" piece of cheesecloth and place the bay leaves, peppercorns, coriander, thyme, and parsley stems in the center. Bring up the ends of the cheesecloth and tie with butchers twine. Place the sachet in the pot and tie one end of the twine to the handle of the pot. Place the pot over high heat and bring to a boil. Reduce the heat to a simmer and cook for one hour. Remove the turkey and remove the meat from the bones. Cut the turkey into bite sized pieces. Reserve the turkey meat and set aside. Return the bones to the stock and continue to reduce the stock by half. Strain, reserving the liquid.

In a large Dutch oven (preferably cast iron) heat the oil over high heat. Add the flour while whisking to create a roux. Cook until the roux turns peanut butter color then reduce the heat to medium. Continue cooking until a light brown color is achieved. Immediately add the onions, celery, and bell pepper while stirring. Cook until the vegetables are soft and the onions are translucent. Add the garlic, bay leaves, and andouille and stir for 2 minutes. Increase the heat to medium-high and add 3 quarts of turkey stock. Bring to a boil then reduce the heat to a simmer. Stir in the thyme and cook for 30 minutes. When ready to serve, add the oysters, 2 cups of reserved turkey meat, salt and pepper, hot sauce, parsley and green onions. Just before serving, remove from heat and stir in 2 tablespoons of filé.

Pass the remaining file at the table. Serve with hot rice.

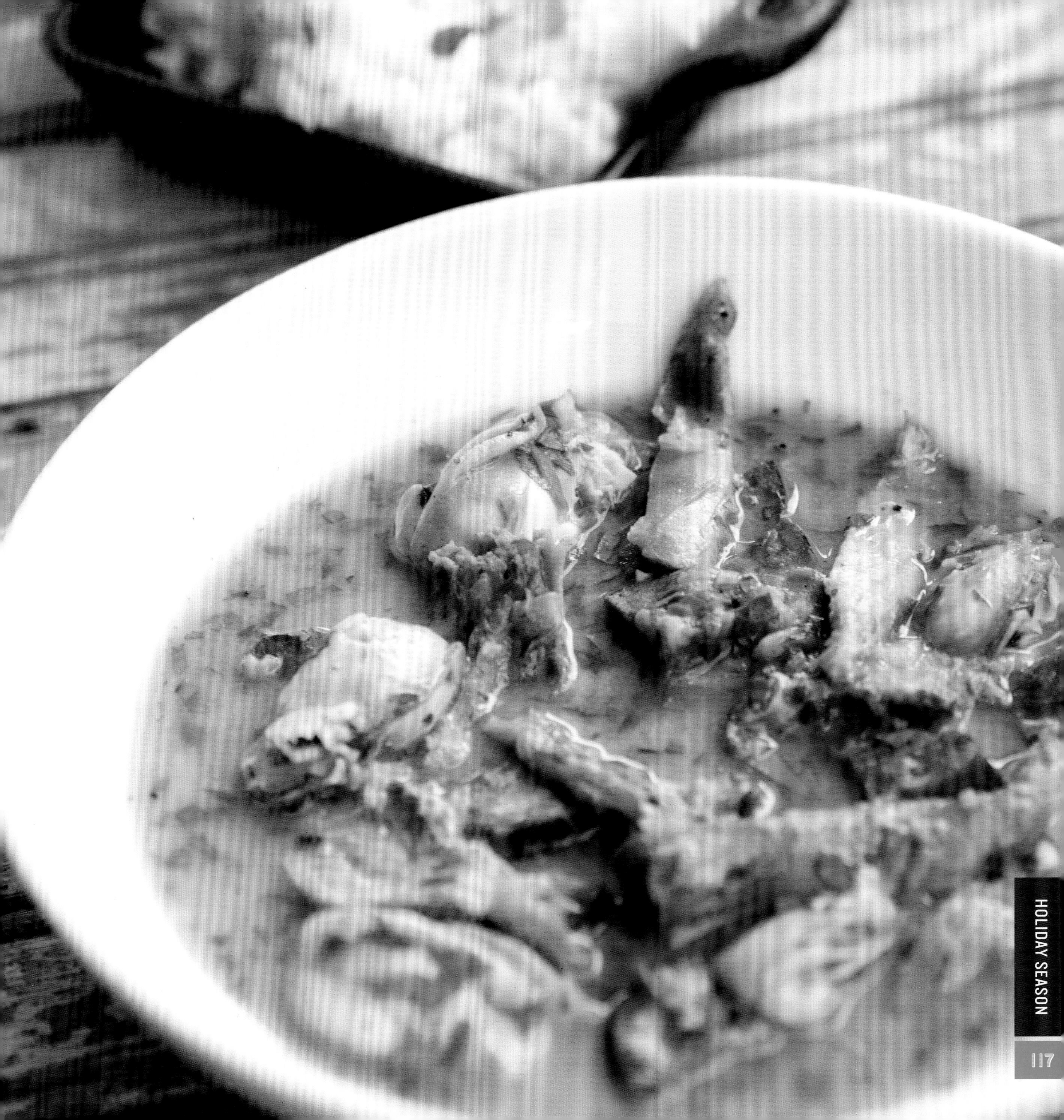

ROASTED BEET SALAD

with Baby Greens and Goat Cheese

— *Serves 4* —

12 baby beets, stems removed

1 tablespoon olive oil

sea salt to taste

fresh ground black pepper to taste

¼ cup sherry vinegar

2 teaspoons Dijon mustard

2 teaspoons shallots

1 teaspoon thyme

1 teaspoon sea salt

½ teaspoon fresh ground black pepper

1 teaspoon honey

¾ cup olive oil

8 cups baby greens

1 cup goat cheese, crumbled

½ cup walnut pieces, toasted

CHEF'S NOTES

I've never heard someone at our family table say "hey, could you pass the beets?" Then I started preparing this salad and that changed. The flavor combination of the roasted beet and the goat cheese is a 1+1=3. Experiment with different color beets for a great looking holiday dish.

Preheat the oven to 350° F. Wash the beets and place on a large sheet of aluminum foil. Drizzle with 1 tablespoon of olive oil and season with salt and pepper. Close the foil to form a pouch, set the pouch on a cookie sheet, and place in the oven. Roast for an hour and fifteen minutes. Remove from the oven and open the pouch. The beets should be easily pierced with a small knife. When cool enough the handle, rub the skin off the beets with a small towel. It helps to wear gloves as beet juice is hard to get off of your hands. Cut the beets into quarters and set aside.

In a small mixing bowl, whisk together the sherry vinegar, mustard, shallots, thyme, salt, pepper, and honey. While whisking, slowly add the olive oil in a slow steady stream.

Add 2 tablespoons of the dressing to the beets and mix well. In a large mixing bowl, toss the arugula with the remaining dressing.

Divide the arugula evenly onto 4 plates. Divide the beets onto the plates of arugula.

Top with the goat cheese and walnuts.

SOUS VIDE TURKEY

Serves 8-10

10 - 12 pound turkey

1 ½ gallon water

1 ½ cups sea salt

1 cup light brown sugar

1 head of garlic, skin removed and cloves smashed

fresh thyme

sea salt to taste

fresh ground black pepper to taste

2 sticks of butter, cut into parts

olive oil

CHEF'S NOTES

In the kitchen, I always love a great gadget. Sous Vide has become a go to cooking technique in my kitchen. Sous Vide machines have revolutionized cooking. Through the use of a water bath and an immersion circulator machine you can precisely regulate your cooking temperature which ensures you never undercook or overcook anything again. You can find Sous Vide machines at high end kitchen retailers.

Remove the giblets from the skin where the neck was and remove the neck from the cavity of the turkey. Rinse the turkey with cold water and pat dry. Cut the wish bone out from the top of the breast. Remove the wings and set aside. Remove the leg and thigh quarter from the carcass and set aside. Cut the breast away by cutting down each side of the breast bone and set aside. Whisk the water, salt, and sugar together until dissolved. Place the turkey pieces in the brine and refrigerate overnight. Reserve the turkey carcass, neck, and giblets for gravy.

Remove the turkey from the brine and pat dry. Season the turkey on all sides with salt and pepper. Place each piece of turkey in its own vacuum bag and add a garlic clove, a sprig of thyme and a pat of butter to the bag. Vacuum on the highest setting. Using an immersion circulator, preheat your water to 160° F. Place the turkey leg and thigh portions in the water bath and cook for 4 hours. Reduce the temperature to 147° F, then add the breast portions and cook an additional 2 hours.

Place a non-stick skillet over medium-high heat. Add the olive oil to the pan and remove the turkey from the bags and dry with a paper towel. Sear the turkey, skin side down, until the skin is brown and crispy. Turn the turkey over to brown on all sides. Keep warm until ready to slice.

ROASTED TURKEY

Serves 10-12

2 gallons water

2 cups sea salt

½ cup honey

12 bay leaves

1 cup garlic cloves, smashed

4 tablespoons black peppercorns

4 tablespoons coriander seeds

1 cup fresh rosemary leaves

1 cup fresh thyme leaves

1 cup fresh parsley leaves

4 oranges

1 turkey, 12-15 pounds, neck and giblets removed

1 stick of butter, softened

sea salt and fresh ground black pepper to taste

4 tablespoons Creole seasoning *(page 166)*

4 onions, peeled and sliced

4 ribs celery, sliced

4 carrots, peeled and chopped

12 cloves garlic, smashed

4 bay leaves

6 sprigs fresh thyme

2 sweet potatoes, peeled and cut into 1" cubes

2 cups white wine

CHEF'S NOTES

The trick to a great juicy turkey with crisp skin is brining the turkey before cooking and basting the skin as it cooks.

Make a sachet using cheesecloth with the bay leaves, garlic, peppercorns, coriander, rosemary, thyme, parsley, and oranges. Tie closed with cotton twine. Fill a large stockpot with 1 gallon of water and set over high heat. Add the sachet and tie the loose end of the twine to the handle of the pot for easy retrieval. Add the salt and honey and bring to a boil. Continue to boil for 5 minutes. Remove from heat and add 1 gallon of ice water. When the brine is completely cooled, add the turkey and refrigerate for 6 hours or overnight. I often use a small ice chest for this.

Preheat the oven to 350° F. Remove the turkey and pat dry. Spread the softened butter between the skin of the turkey breast and the meat. Season inside the cavity and the outside of the turkey with salt and pepper. Then season with the Creole seasoning. Use extra seasoning inside the cavity. Place half of the onions, celery, carrots, garlic, bay leaves, thyme, and sweet potatoes inside the cavity. Using cotton twine, tie the legs closed. Place the remaining half of the vegetables in the bottom of a roasting pan. Set the turkey on top of the vegetables so it is not in contact with the pan. Add the wine to the bottom of the roasting pan then cover the pan with aluminum foil, sealing tightly. Bake for about 3 hours. Remove the foil and baste with the juices that have been released. Return to the oven uncovered and cook until the turkey thigh reaches 160° F, basting every 5 minutes. Remove from the oven and allow to rest for 30 minutes. The residual heat should bring the turkey to an internal temperature of 165° F. Follow the gravy instructions or pour the juices into a blender with some of the roasted vegetables and purée. Add more roasted vegetables for a thicker sauce.

TURKEY STOCK & GRAVY

Makes 1 Quart

For the Stock:

turkey carcass and neck

2 tablespoons olive oil

2 tablespoons butter

reserved turkey giblets

1 cup onion, peeled and chopped

½ cup carrot, peeled and chopped

½ cup celery, chopped

4 cloves garlic, smashed

1 cup dry white wine

6 cups water

parsley stems from one bunch of parsley

6 sprigs of fresh thyme

2 bay leaves

2 cloves

1 tablespoon black peppercorns

1 tablespoon coriander seeds

For the Gravy:

½ stick of butter

⅓ cup flour

2 cups white wine

reserved turkey stock

sea salt and fresh ground black pepper to taste

2 teaspoons fresh thyme

2 tablespoons butter

For the Stock:

Preheat the oven to 350 degrees F. Place the turkey carcass, neck, and giblets on a sheet pan and drizzle with the olive oil. Place in the oven and roast for an hour.

Meanwhile, melt the butter in a large stockpot over medium-high heat. Add the onions, carrots, celery, and garlic and sauté until the vegetables are light brown, about 10 minutes. Add the wine and cook for 2 minutes, then add the water and roasted turkey carcass, neck, and giblets. Bring to a boil and reduce heat to a simmer. Add the parsley, thyme, bay leaves, cloves, peppercorns, and coriander and simmer for 1 ½ hours. Strain the broth and cool.

For the Gravy:

In a large stockpot over medium-high heat, melt the butter. Stir in the flour while whisking and make a light brown roux. Add the wine and stir with a whisk to make a thickened sauce. Add the stock and bring to a boil, then reduce the heat to a simmer. Season with salt, pepper, and thyme. When ready to serve, remove from heat and whisk in the butter to emulsify.

PAW-PAW'S OYSTER DRESSING

Yields 2 Gallons

1 cup butter

10 cups onions, peeled and chopped

5 bay leaves

½ cup garlic, minced

2 bunches green onions, sliced

1 bunch fresh Italian parsley, chopped

1 pound cooked pork sausage, hot or spicy
(I use Jimmy Dean)

1 gallon oysters, chopped, liquid reserved

1 ½ loaves of stale New Orleans style French bread,
cut into 2" cubes

1 cup seasoned Italian bread crumbs

Louisiana hot sauce to taste

1 tablespoon fresh thyme

sea salt to taste

fresh ground black pepper to taste

CHEF'S NOTES

Nothing makes it feel more like holiday season than cooking my grandfather's oyster dressing recipe. After years of trying to reproduce it, I finally learned the secret and I will share it with you. If you can find them, use unwashed oysters. You want that great salt taste to add flavor to your dressing.

Preheat an oven to 350° F.

Melt the butter in a large pot over medium-high heat. Sauté the onions, bay leaves, and garlic until soft (about 5 – 10 minutes). Add the green onions and parsley and cook for 1 minute. Add chopped oysters gradually, as not to reduce the heat so the oysters do not become watery.

In a separate pan cook the sausage, drain the rendered fat, and add to mix. Cover the pot and lower the heat and cook for 15 minutes for the flavors to blend.

Meanwhile, soak the French bread in reserved oyster water, working it with your hands to get full absorption. Add the bread a little at a time to achieve a thick consistency. Remove from heat.

Add the breadcrumbs, hot sauce, and thyme and stir until well mixed. Season to taste with salt and pepper.

Place in an uncovered baking pan *(casserole dish)* and bake for 30 minutes or until hot and bubbly.

ABITA™ ROOT BEER GLAZED HAM

Serves 8-10

1 large ham, 8 - 10 pounds

3 bottles Abita™ Root Beer

1 ½ cup honey

¾ cup Creole mustard

1 cup pineapple juice

½ teaspoon ground cloves

1 stick cinnamon

1 teaspoon fresh ground black pepper

Preheat the oven to 350° F.

Place the ham in a large roasting pan and cover with aluminum foil and bake for 30 minutes.

Meanwhile, in a saucepan, combine the Abita™ Root Beer, honey, Creole mustard, pineapple juice, cloves, cinnamon, and pepper and bring to a boil.

Reduce the heat to a simmer and reduce by half. After 30 minutes, remove the foil and add half the glaze.

Continue to bake uncovered for another hour. Baste every 15 minutes.

Serve the ham with the reserved glaze on the side.

BOURBON PECAN PIE

Serves 12

1 ½ cups pecans

¾ cup semisweet chocolate chips

1 unbaked 9-inch pie shell

4 eggs, beaten

½ cup sugar

½ cup light brown sugar

½ cup light corn syrup

2 tablespoons bourbon

½ teaspoon vanilla extract

pinch salt

Preheat the oven to 300° F.

Spread the pecan pieces and the chocolate chips evenly on the bottom of the pie shell. In a mixing bowl, whisk the remaining ingredients together. Pour the filling over the pecans.

Bake for about 1 hour or until the filling sets.

Cool for 30 minutes before slicing.

Cut into individual servings and serve with a scoop of vanilla ice cream.

HUNTING SEASON

HUNTING

Hunting, like boiling a pot of crawfish, is a rite of passage for a young man growing up in Louisiana. As a child, I remember learning how to hunt by going with my Dad on dove and squirrel hunts, then I would later graduate on to rabbits, then my favorite, duck hunting. I never was much of a deer hunter, I felt there wasn't enough action.

Growing up I would go hunting after school, it was a way of life. Hunting is about the sport, however, like fishing, it is also very much about the story of your hunt. Every Monday morning when coming back to school, all my friends would share stories of what they saw and what they conquered that weekend.

The best memories I have of hunting come from Thanksgiving day with my dad and brother.

We would traditionally go duck hunting before our Thanksgiving Day lunch and then spend the evening relaxing. Not only was this a great time but I always knew that with Thanksgiving the busiest time of year began the next day, Christmas season. That hunt on Thanksgiving morning and lunch later that day was extra special because I knew it was the last time I would be able to spend quality time with my family for the next several weeks.

Like Fishing Season, this chapter has great recipes that you can easily substitute for most wild game after your hunt. Enjoy your hunting, but most importantly, enjoy the stories you create. You'll tell them for a lifetime.

ALLIGATOR SAUSAGE

Makes 20 Links

2 ½ pounds alligator meat

2 ½ pounds pork shoulder

½ cup onions, peeled and chopped

¼ cup celery, chopped

¼ cup red bell pepper, seeded and chopped

2 tablespoons garlic, minced

¼ cup fresh Italian parsley, chopped

½ cup green onion, sliced

1 tablespoon fresh thyme, chopped

1 tablespoon coriander, ground

½ tablespoon crushed red pepper

2 tablespoons sea salt

15 feet sausage casing

CHEF'S NOTES

I have to be honest, it's hard to get Louisiana Alligator in stores because of the success of the show "Swamp People." I've included my best references for sourcing great ingredients on page 174. In general, alligator meat does tend be pretty tough which is why it is great to use for sausage. This recipe will also work for other wild game after your hunt.

It is important when making sausage to keep all of the ingredients as cold as possible.

Mix all of the ingredients except the casing in a large mixing bowl. Add 1 cup of ice and mix well. Grind in a meat grinder then stuff into the sausage casing if desired. Tie the links off at 6" intervals.

Preheat an oven to 350° F.

Place the links in a baking pan and add ¼" of water. Place in the oven and bake for 20 minutes.

Turn the sausage every 5 minutes, adding more water as it evaporates.

Serve with spicy mustard sauce.

WILD BOAR TAMALES

Yields 24 Tamales

Filling:

8 large ancho chiles, stemmed, seeded, and chopped

1 tablespoon garlic, chopped

1 teaspoon fresh ground black pepper

1 teaspoon coriander, ground

½ teaspoon cumin, ground

3 cups water

1 ½ pounds wild boar shoulder
(or pork shoulder), cut into ½" cubes

1 teaspoon sea salt to taste

Batter:

1 ⅓ cups lard (or Crisco)

2 teaspoons sea salt

½ teaspoon baking powder

3 ½ cups masa harina

4 cups chicken stock, simmering *(page 167)*

1 package corn husks

In a blender, combine the chilies, garlic, pepper and cumin. Add the water and blend to a smooth purée. Strain into a saucepan, add the meat, 3 cups of water, and the salt. Simmer uncovered over medium heat for one hour or until the meat is tender and the sauce has reduced. Strain the meat from the sauce and break the boar into small pieces and taste for seasoning. Allow to cool to room temperature.

In an electric mixer on medium-high beat the lard, salt, and baking powder until light in texture, about 1 minute. Combine the masa and 2 cups of stock in a mixing bowl and whisk together. Add to the electric mixer and blend on medium low. Slowly add in 1 cup of chicken stock. Slowly mix for another minute or so adding more stock if necessary. Refrigerate the batter for an hour, then re-mix when ready to stuff.

While the meat cooks, put the corn husks in a large bowl and submerge in hot water.

Remove a corn husk from the hot water and pat dry with a towel. Lay the long side facing you. Spread about ⅓ cup of batter into a rectangular shape. Take 2 tablespoons of meat mixture and lay down the center of the tamale batter. Take the corn husk on the near side and fold over to cover the meat mixture and continue folding into a log shape. Fold the end in and finish and lay, folded side down, in the steamer rack.

Set up your steamer and steam the tamales about 20 minutes. Serve with the braising sauce on the side.

DUCK BOUDIN

Makes 50 Links

2 ½ pounds duck meat cut into 1" cubes

2 ½ pounds pork shoulder cut into 1" cubes

¾ pounds chicken or pork liver, 1" cubes

1 ½ large onions, peeled and chopped

2 ribs of celery, chopped

4 jalapeños, seeded and chopped

¼ cup garlic, chopped

5 tablespoons sea salt

1 tablespoon fresh ground black pepper

1 tablespoon ground white pepper

½ tablespoon curing salt

½ tablespoon cayenne pepper

½ tablespoon chili powder

1 gallon chicken stock *(page 167)*

10 cups cooked rice

2 tablespoons fresh thyme, chopped

1 cup fresh Italian parsley, chopped

1 ½ cups green onions, sliced

2 packages of natural casings

CHEF'S NOTES

Boudin is a type of a Cajun sausage traditionally made with rice and pork. In my recipe I add one of my favorite wild game meats, duck, for a really great boudin, especially duck legs. Also, be sure to use pork shoulder to give the boudin a really moist flavor.

Combine the duck, pork, liver, onions, celery, jalapeños, garlic, salts, peppers, and chili powder and marinate overnight in the refrigerator. Place the marinated mixture in a large pot and cover with the chicken stock. Bring the mixture to a boil and reduce the heat to a simmer. Cook for 1 hour until tender. Remove from heat and strain, reserving the liquid. Allow to cool slightly and pass through a meat grinder with a coarse die. Place in a large bowl and add the rice, thyme, parsley, green onions, and reserved cooking liquid; mix well. Stuff into casings and poach in simmering water (not boiling) for 10 minutes.

ROASTED QUAIL SALAD
with Creole Mustard and Cane Syrup Vinaigrette

Serves 4

4 quail, semi boneless

2 tablespoons Creole seasoning *(page 166)*

2 tablespoons olive oil

2 tablespoons butter

6 cups mixed baby greens

½ red onion, peeled and sliced thin

½ cup Feta cheese, crumbled

½ cup dried cranberries

½ cup pecan pieces, roasted

½ cup cherry tomatoes, halved

¼ cup green onions, sliced

1 teaspoon garlic, minced

¼ cup Steen's cane vinegar

2 tablespoons Creole mustard

¼ cup + 1 tablespoon Steen's cane syrup

1 cup olive oil

sea salt to taste

fresh ground black pepper to taste

Preheat an oven to 350° F. Season the quail on each side with Creole seasoning. Heat the olive oil and butter in a large sauté pan over medium-high heat. When the butter is melted and bubbling, add the quail breast side down. Cook for 4 minutes until golden brown. Turn the quail over and immediately place the pan in the oven. Cook for 5 minutes then remove from the oven, baste with the melted butter, and allow to rest for 5 minutes.

In a large salad bowl, combine the baby greens, red onion, Feta cheese, cranberries, pecans, tomatoes, and green onions.

In a small container, combine the garlic, cane vinegar, Creole mustard, cane syrup and olive oil. Blend with an immersion blender, season with salt and pepper and blend again.

Toss the greens with the vinaigrette and divide onto 4 plates. Top each salad with a roasted quail.

HUNTER'S CASSOULET

Serves 12

1 tablespoon olive oil

4 rabbit hind legs

4 duck legs

2 pound venison roast, cut into 2" pieces

sea salt and fresh ground black pepper to taste

4 slices of bacon, diced

1 smoked ham hock

1 cup onion, peeled and chopped

½ cup celery, chopped

½ cup carrots, peeled and chopped

1 tablespoon garlic, chopped

½ pound andouille sausage, sliced into ¼" slices

½ cup dry white wine

1 cup canned diced tomatoes with their juice

1 (32 ounce) can of navy beans, drained and rinsed

8 ounces beef stock

1 bay leaf

1 tablespoon fresh thyme, chopped

¾ tablespoon fresh rosemary, chopped

1 tablespoon Creole seasoning *(page 166)*

Topping

1 cup bread crumbs

1 stick butter, melted

¼ cup Parmesan cheese, grated

1 tablespoon Creole seasoning *(page 166)*

CHEF'S NOTES

This is a great utilitarian recipe for any outdoorsman. You can use any wild game you like, in fact, this is one of those recipes that is great to put together on a fall weekend to clean out your freezer of different wild game meats you're not quite sure what to do with. This recipe brings all those great flavors together.

In a large braising pan or Dutch oven heat the olive oil over medium-high heat. Season the rabbit, duck, and venison with salt and pepper. Add the game and sear for 4 minutes or until golden brown.

Remove the rabbit, duck and venison to a plate with a slotted spoon. Add the diced bacon and the ham hock and sauté until the bacon has rendered some of its fat and is beginning to crisp. Add the onions, celery, and carrots and cook until the onions turn clear, about 5 minutes. Add the garlic and stir for 1 minute. Add the andouille and cook for 2 minutes.

Deglaze with white wine scraping up any browned bits from the bottom of the pan. Add the tomatoes, beans, stock, and reserved meats. Bring to a boil and reduce heat to a simmer. Add the herbs and season with salt and pepper. Simmer for 20 minutes.

Preheat the oven to 350° F.

Mix all of the topping ingredients together in a mixing bowl. Pour the cassoulet into a casserole dish and spread the topping evenly over the cassoulet. Bake uncovered for 20 minutes.

RABBIT RAGU

⊢ *Serves 6* ⊣

1 rabbit, cut into 8 pieces

2 tablespoons of balsamic vinegar

1 tablespoon Creole seasoning *(page 166)*

¼ cup olive oil

1 cup onion, peeled and chopped

½ cup celery, chopped

½ cup carrot, peeled and chopped

1 tablespoon garlic, chopped

1 cup red wine

4 cups roasted chicken stock

1 bay leaf

5 sprigs of fresh thyme

1 sprig rosemary

1 tablespoon coriander seed, ground

1 tablespoon black peppercorns, ground

½ pound smoked bacon, chopped

2 cups wild mushrooms, sliced

2 tablespoons fresh Italian parsley, chopped

2 tablespoons green onions, sliced

sea salt and fresh ground black pepper to taste

2 tablespoons butter

6 cups gnocchi

½ cup freshly grated Parmesan cheese

In a large mixing bowl, add the rabbit and the balsamic vinegar and marinate for 15 minutes. Heat the olive oil in a large pot over medium-high heat. Remove the rabbit from the marinade, reserving the marinade. Season the rabbit with Creole seasoning and add to the hot oil. Do not crowd the rabbit, turn and brown the rabbit on all sides and then remove from the pot and set aside to cool. Add the onions, celery, and carrots to the hot oil scraping any browned bit of rabbit in the pan. Cook for about 5 minutes or until softened. Add the garlic and stir for 1 minute, then deglaze with the red wine, scraping the bottom of the pan. Add the chicken stock, bay leaf, thyme, rosemary, coriander and peppercorns. Bring to a boil and reduce the heat to a simmer. Add the rabbit back to the sauce and braise for about 10 minutes. This should be just enough to cook the rabbit through. Do not allow to boil or the rabbit will be tough.

Remove the rabbit again and cool. When cool enough to handle, separate the rabbit meat from the bones. Cut the boneless meat into bite sized pieces and reserve in the refrigerator. Add the bones to the pot and continue to simmer for an hour longer. Remove the sauce from the heat and strain it to remove the bones and seasonings.

In a new pot, add the bacon and render until it is crisp. Add the mushrooms and stir for about 2 minutes. Add the reserved stock and bring to a simmer. Reduce until the sauce coats the back of a spoon. Add the parsley, green onions, and rabbit meat and heat through. Season to taste with salt and pepper.

Melt the butter in a large non-stick sauté pan over medium-high heat. Add the gnocchi and sauté until golden brown on each side. Add the sauce and rabbit to the gnocchi. Divide into 6 pasta bowls and garnish with the Parmesan cheese.

145

PAN ROASTED VENISON MEDALLIONS

with Blackberry Sauce and Celery Root Purée

Serves 4

1 cup port wine

½ cup blackberry jelly

2 cups veal demi-glace

1 pint fresh blackberries

sea salt and fresh ground black pepper to taste

2 tablespoons + 2 tablespoons butter

2 tablespoons olive oil

1 tablespoon juniper berries

1 tablespoon coriander seeds

1 tablespoon fennel seeds

1 tablespoon white peppercorns

1 tablespoon sea salt

8 venison medallions, about 3 ounces each

2 cups Celery Root Purée *(page 167)*

Bring the port wine to a boil in a sauce pot over medium-high heat. Reduce the heat to a simmer and reduce the port by half.

Add the blackberry jelly and veal demi-glace and cook while stirring to dissolve the jelly. Reduce until the sauce coats the back of a spoon, about 5 minutes. Season with salt and pepper.

Remove from heat and whisk in 2 tablespoons of butter. Keep warm until ready to serve.

Preheat the oven to 350° F.

In a spice grinder, blend the juniper, coriander, fennel, and peppercorns to a fine powder. Add to the salt and season the venison medallions on all sides.

Heat the olive oil and butter in a large skillet over medium-high heat. Place the venison medallions in the sauté pan and sear until golden brown on the first side, about 2 minutes. Turn the venison and place the pan in the oven. Cook for 6 - 8 minutes or until medium rare.

Place ½ cup of celery root purée on each plate and top with 2 venison medallions and 2 tablespoons of the blackberry sauce.

TAILGATING SEASON

I t's probably every Louisianian's favorite time of year. The summer heat begins to break, the air feels a little bit dryer (just a little) and you know what's around the corner: Football! It simply doesn't get any better than fall in the south. Everything just feels right. It's also the busiest time of the year, and as the season kicks off, the busiest time at our restaurants is upon us. It seems like one minute you're cheering on the Tigers and Saints in their home openers and, before you know it, you're wrapping Christmas gifts to put under the tree. The energy during this time of year is positively electric.

Nothing beats a great tailgate party, whether it's for the Tigers, the Ragin' Cajuns, the Saints or whichever team you support. Tailgating is a way of life in Louisiana.

Ruffin Rodrigue, my business partner in our restaurants, was an All American offensive lineman for LSU in the 1980s.

He even played in the historic "Earthquake Game." Our love of football is on full display in many of the artifacts that adorn our restaurant. And you'll often find the crew from ESPN, CBS or ABC at Ruffino's the night before a big game in Death Valley.

In the following pages, you'll find several classic recipes to satisfy all your hungry tailgating friends; but I recommend you make enough to share with fans that pass by, too...because once they see and smell what you've made, they'll come begging!

Some of these recipes are great for cooking on-site, and others you can even prepare ahead of time to avoid the stress of gameday. I've also included a few recipes that you can enjoy at home when you decide to stay put and watch the game on the flat screen. No matter where you're cheering on your favorite team, these recipes, and a group of crazy fans, are all you need. Geaux Tigers!

CHICKEN & ANDOUILLE JAMBALAYA

Serves 16-20

1 cup bacon drippings (or Crisco)

5 pounds chicken thighs

3 tablespoons Creole seasoning *(page 166)*

1 ½ pounds andouille, sliced into ¼" rounds

3 onions, peeled and chopped

2 ribs of celery, chopped

2 green bell peppers, stemmed, seeded and chopped

1 tablespoon garlic, chopped

4 cups rice

8 cups chicken stock

2 bay leaves

2 tablespoons fresh thyme, chopped

½ cup fresh Italian parsley, chopped

½ cup green onions, sliced

Creole seasoning *(page 166)*, sea salt and fresh ground black pepper to taste

Louisiana hot sauce to taste

CHEF'S NOTES

There are many opinions on where the word "jambalaya" originated. The story I tell is that it derives from a combination of the French 'jambon,' meaning ham, the French article 'à la,' or "in the style of," and 'ya,' meaning rice. The dish itself has its roots in the classic Spanish staple, paella. We southerners have modified it to make it uniquely our own. There are two major variations: Creole jambalaya, which uses tomato and is more red in color; and the Cajun version, which does not include tomato. I prefer the Cajun version.

Remove the bones from the chicken thighs and cut the chicken into 1" cubes. The bones can be added to the stock. Heat the bacon drippings in a large Dutch oven (preferably cast iron) over medium-high heat. Season the chicken with the Creole seasoning. Add the chicken to the pan and cook until well browned. The more brown you get the chicken the more brown the jambalaya will be. Remove the chicken and set aside. Add the andouille and cook until golden brown. Remove the andouille and set aside. Add the onions and cook until they are light brown. Stir in the celery and green bell pepper and cook for 5 minutes. Add the garlic and cook 1 minute longer. Add the rice and cook while stirring for 1 minute. Add the chicken stock, chicken pieces andouille, bay leaves, and thyme. Bring to a boil then reduce the heat to low and cover. Allow to cook undisturbed for 20 minutes. Remove the lid, add the parsley and green onions and adjust the seasoning with the Creole seasoning, salt, pepper, and hot sauce. Don't stir, but fold from the bottom up in 4 or 5 different spots. Replace the cover, turn off the heat and allow to rest for 15 minutes.

SHRIMP & TASSO PASTA

Serves 6

1 pound of fettuccine

sea salt

2 tablespoons butter

¾ cups tasso, diced

½ cup onion, peeled and chopped

1 tablespoon garlic, chopped

36 - 40 large Gulf shrimp, peeled and deveined

2 tablespoons Creole seasoning *(page 166)*

1 tablespoon fresh thyme, chopped

½ cup white wine

2 cups heavy whipping cream

½ cup Pecorino Romano cheese, grated

½ cup green onions, sliced

¼ cup fresh Italian parsley, chopped

2 tablespoons butter

sea salt to taste

fresh ground black pepper to taste

CHEF'S NOTES

Tasso is a heavily seasoned piece of pork that I like to use as a seasoning ingredient, rather than as a main protein. Tasso adds a delicious smoky and spicy flavor to the pasta.

Bring a large pot of water to a boil seasoned heavily with salt. It should taste like the ocean. Add the fettuccine and stir. Cook according to package directions until al dente, soft but firm to the bite. Drain.

Meanwhile, heat the butter in a large sauté pan over medium-high heat.

Add the tasso and cook for 2 minutes. Add the onions and cook 2 more minutes. Stir in the garlic and cook 1 minute longer.

Season the shrimp with Creole seasoning and cook until they just begin to turn pink.

Deglaze with white wine, add the thyme, and reduce by half, about 2 minutes. Add the cream and cook 2 minutes more. Stir in the Romano cheese, green onions, and parsley.

Add the pasta and butter until the butter has emulsified. Season to taste with salt and pepper and divide into 6 bowls.

Serve hot.

SEAFOOD OKRA GUMBO

Yields 2 ½ Gallons

1 cup butter

1 ½ cups flour

2 onions, peeled and chopped

2 green bell pepper, seeded and chopped

4 celery stalks, chopped

¼ cup garlic, minced

1 pound okra, sliced

1 pound andouille, halved lengthwise
and sliced into ¼" slices

1 quart San Marzano tomatoes,
chopped with juices

¼ cup filé powder

4 bay leaves

1 teaspoon fresh ground black pepper

½ teaspoon cayenne pepper, ground

½ teaspoon white pepper, ground

1 tablespoon fresh thyme, chopped

5 quarts seafood stock

3 pounds gumbo crabs

2 ½ pounds Gulf shrimp, peeled and deveined

1 quart shucked oysters

1 pound claw crab meat

Louisiana hot sauce to taste

Worcestershire sauce to taste

½ cup fresh Italian Parsley, chopped

½ cup green onions, sliced

hot steamed rice

CHEF'S NOTES

I like to look at gumbo as a food analogy for south Louisiana. The best gumbo is a blend of all the cooking methods and ingredients inspired by the French, Italian, Spanish, and German cultures that make our state so unique. Nothing says classic Louisiana more than a hot pot of gumbo and football in the fall.

In a large stockpot over high heat melt the butter.

Stir in the flour and stir to make a dark roux (mahogany colored). Stir in the onions, celery, and bell pepper and cook until the onions turn clear. Stir in the garlic and okra and cook for 5 minutes. Stir in the andouille and tomatoes and cook for 5 minutes more.

Mix in the filé, bay leaves, peppers, and thyme. Whisk in the stock and bring to a boil. Reduce the heat to a simmer and cook for one hour.

Skim the top as necessary. Stir in the seafood, hot sauce, and Worcestershire, and cook until the seafood is cooked through.

Remove from heat and add the green onions and parsley.

Serve over hot steamed rice.

MUFFALETTA

Yields 24 Muffalettas

Olive Salad:

1 cup black olives, pitted

1 cup green olives, pitted

¼ cup red onion, peeled and chopped

¼ cup celery, chopped

2 tablespoons garlic, chopped

¼ cup green onions, chopped

¼ cup fresh Italian parsley, chopped

1 tablespoon oregano

1 cup extra virgin olive oil

¼ cup red wine vinegar

1 teaspoon fresh ground black pepper

Muffaletta:

24 small Italian rolls
(sesame seeds preferable)

24 slices ham

24 slices Genoa salami

24 slices provolone cheese

6 slices mortadella, cut into quarters

CHEF'S NOTES

If you're eating a muffaletta at a restaurant, there's a good chance that the bread comes from United Bakery in New Orleans. They are the authority for muffaletta bread. If you can't get your bread from United Bakery, then fear not. Pick up any Italian bread with sesame seeds and you'll be good to go. Serve it up hot or cold; whatever you prefer. As a native New Orleanian, I probably shouldn't admit it... but I love my muffalettas warmed in the oven before serving.

Combine all of the olive salad ingredients in a food processor. Pulse several times to get a course consistency.

Store in an airtight container. It will hold for 2 weeks refrigerated.

For a muffaletta, on Italian bread, place sliced ham, Genoa salami, mortadella, provolone cheese, and olive salad.

The key to a good muffaletta is to let the bread soak up the seasoned olive oil from the olive salad.

It is not traditional, but muffalettas can be warmed in the oven.

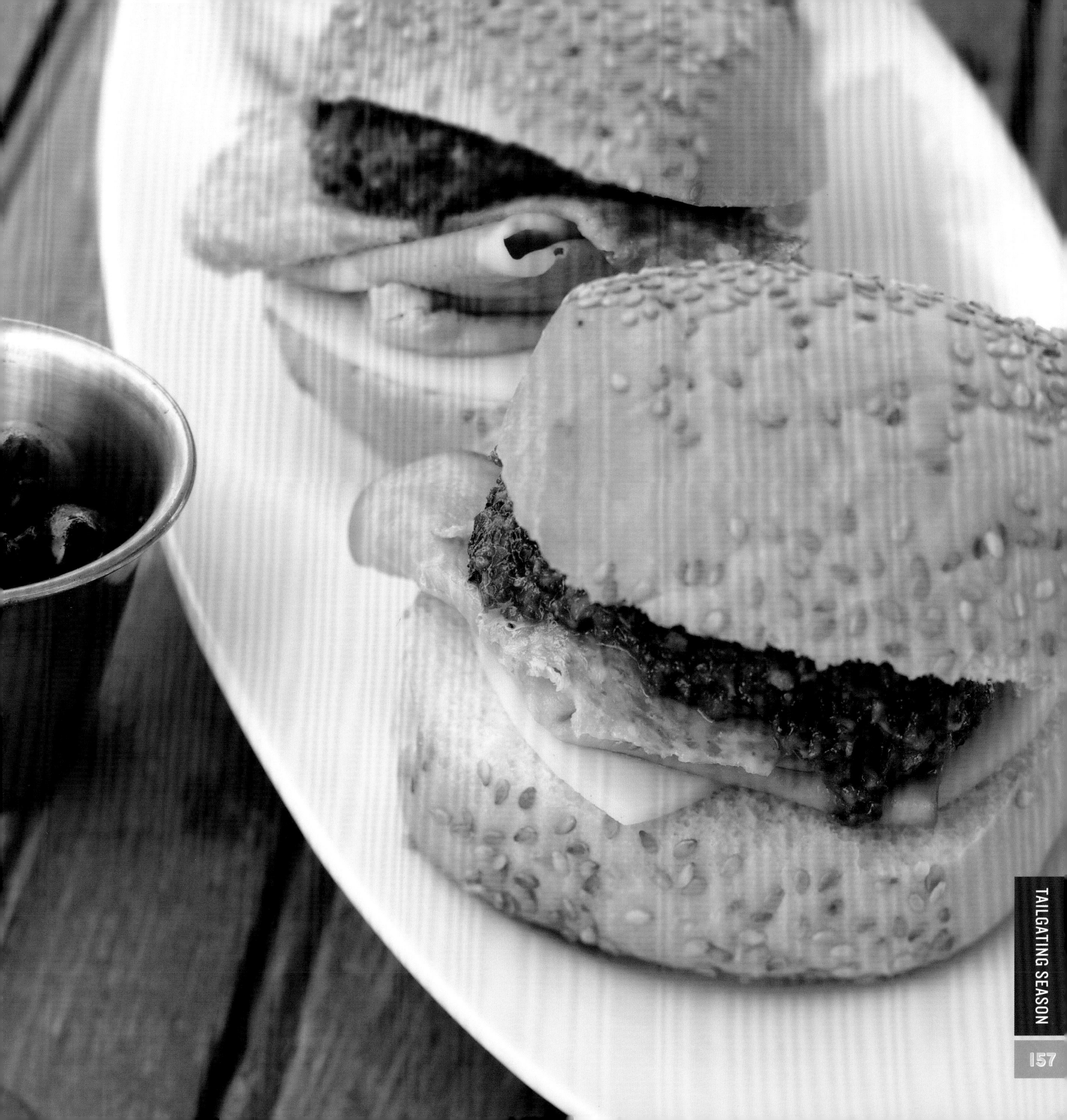

BAYOU WINGS

Serves 4

½ cup Louisiana hot sauce

1 tablespoon garlic, chopped

¼ cup heavy whipping cream

1 stick butter

vegetable oil for frying

2 pounds frog legs

2 tablespoons + 2 tablespoons Creole seasoning *(page 166)*

2 cups flour

½ cup olive oil

3 radishes, trimmed and thinly sliced

1 stalk celery, thinly sliced on a bias

1 small bunch of cilantro, leaves picked

juice of one lime

sea salt and fresh ground black pepper to taste

Truffled Ranch Dressing *(page 166)*

In a small saucepan combine the hot sauce with the garlic. Cook over medium heat until reduced by half. Stir in the cream and reduce for a couple of minutes more.

Lower the heat and whisk in the butter a little at a time until it is emulsified. Reserve in a warm spot.

Preheat the fryer to 350° F.

Season the frog legs with 2 tablespoons Creole seasoning. In a small bowl, mix the flour with the remaining 2 tablespoons of Creole seasoning.

Dredge the frog legs in the seasoned flour then fry until crisp and golden brown. Remove from the fryer and drain on paper towels.

Pour the sauce into a large mixing bowl and add the frog legs, tossing to coat.

In another small bowl combine the radishes, celery, cilantro, lime juice and olive oil. Season with salt and pepper.

Serve with Truffled Ranch Dressing.

SEAFOOD PASTA SALAD

Serves 10

1 cup Creole tomatoes, cored, and seeded

1 cup mayonnaise

½ tablespoon granulated garlic

½ teaspoon sea salt

¼ teaspoon fresh ground black pepper

1 pound orzo pasta

1 tablespoon sea salt

½ cup sun dried tomatoes, diced

½ cup Kalamata olives, quartered lengthwise

½ cup crumbled Feta cheese

½ cup celery, chopped

1 small red onion, peeled and chopped

2 tablespoons fresh oregano, chopped

2 tablespoons fresh Italian parsley, chopped

¼ cup green onions, sliced

½ pound boiled Gulf shrimp, peeled and chopped

½ pound Louisiana crawfish tails, peeled

½ pound jumbo lump crabmeat

sea salt and ground black pepper to taste

CHEF'S NOTES

Looking for an easy dish to make ahead of time for the big game? This is it. It works great as a cold pasta that can even be prepared a few days in advance.

In a blender, combine the tomatoes, mayonnaise, granulated garlic, salt and pepper. Blend until smooth. Set aside.

Bring a large pot of water to a rolling boil. Season the water with sea salt until it tastes like the ocean.

Add the orzo and cook until al dente. Drain and rinse with cold water to stop the cooking and remove some of the starch.

Place in a large mixing bowl. Add the sun dried tomatoes, olives, feta cheese, celery, red onion, oregano, parsley, green onions, shrimp, crawfish, crabmeat, and 1 cup of the tomato dressing and mix well.

CEDAR PLANK REDFISH

Serves 6

6 untreated cedar planks *(8 – 10" long)*

½ cup olive oil

6 6-ounce fillets of fresh fish
*(Redfish, Speckled Trout, or
Salmon work the best)*

2 tablespoons Creole seasoning *(page 166)*

3 Creole tomatoes

1 cup basil pesto *(page 167)*

½ cup balsamic syrup

CHEF'S NOTES

Unfortunately, I can't travel to every LSU and Saints away game each season, and I'm guessing you can't either. This recipe is ideal for throwing on the grill at halftime, and you can take care of all the prep work before the party starts. You can find planks of inexpensive cedar at your local hardware store. Just make sure they're untreated. Soak them in water beforehand so they won't flare up on the grill, and they'll last the entire season.

Soak the cedar planks in water for at least an hour before hand.

Preheat the grill.

Brush the plank with olive oil. Season the fish on both sides with Creole seasoning. Lay the fish in the center of the plank.

Cut the tomato in half, lay it on its side and cut into thin slices. Lay the tomatoes shingle style over the fish, covering the flesh of the fish.

Set the plank in the center of the grill and cover immediately. Cook for about 15 minutes or until the fish is cooked and flaky.

There will be a lot of smoke but this is from the plank smoldering.

Serve the plank on a plate and drizzle with pesto and balsamic syrup.

LAGNIAPPE

*Sauces, Seasonings, Dressings,
and a few things extra*

CREOLE SEASONING

CREOLE MEUNIERE SAUCE

2 ounces demi-glace

1 ounce lemon juice

2 ounces white wine

2 sticks butter, cut in pieces

sea salt to taste

fresh ground white pepper to taste

In a sauté pan over medium heat, bring the demi-glace, lemon juice, and white wine to a boil and reduce by half. Reduce the heat to low. While swirling the pan or whisking, slowly add the butter a piece at a time until it is all incorporated. Season with salt and white pepper.

Makes 1 cup.

NICOISE SALAD DRESSING

2 tablespoons fresh lemon juice

2 tablespoons Steen's cane vinegar
(or red wine vinegar)

2 tablespoons Dijon mustard

1 tablespoon garlic, minced

2 anchovies, minced

¼ cup Parmesan cheese, grated

¾ cup extra virgin olive oil

½ teaspoon sea salt

½ teaspoon fresh ground
black pepper

½ teaspoon granulated sugar

In the bowl of a food processor or blender add the lemon juice, vinegar, Dijon, garlic, anchovy, and cheese. Blend and, with the motor running, slowly pour in the olive oil. Season with salt, pepper, and sugar.

Makes 1 cup.

CREOLE SEASONING

10 tablespoons sea salt

4 tablespoons fresh ground
black pepper

1 teaspoon cayenne pepper, ground

½ teaspoon ground white pepper

4 tablespoons granulated garlic

3 tablespoons granulated onion

2 tablespoons oregano, dried

2 tablespoons thyme, dried

10 tablespoons paprika, ground

Combine all ingredients in a zip lock bag and blend well.

ALFREDO SAUCE

½ cup heavy whipping cream

2 ounces butter, softened

¼ cup Parmigiano-Reggiano, grated

sea salt and fresh ground black pepper

In a skillet over medium-high heat, bring the cream to a boil. Reduce the heat to a simmer and stir in the butter. Keep stirring until the butter is incorporated. Remove from heat and whisk in the cheese until it is melted. Season to taste with salt and pepper.

TRUFFLED RANCH DRESSING

¾ cup mayonnaise

½ cup buttermilk

¼ cup fresh tarragon, chopped

2 tablespoons green onion, chopped

1 tablespoon fresh Italian parsley,
chopped

2 teaspoons garlic, chopped

2 teaspoons fresh squeezed
lemon juice

1 ½ teaspoons granulated garlic

½ teaspoon dried oregano

¼ teaspoon chili powder

1 teaspoon white truffle oil

½ teaspoon truffled salt

Combine all the ingredients in a bowl and whisk until blended.

BASIL PESTO

¼ cup grated Parmesan cheese

¼ cup grated Pecorino Romano

⅓ cup toasted pine nuts

2 cups packed fresh basil leaves

¼ cup fresh Italian parsley

2 teaspoon garlic, chopped

½ teaspoon sea salt

¼ teaspoon fresh ground black pepper

½ cup olive oil

In a small saucepan blanch the basil and parsley in boiling, salted water for 10 seconds. Remove from water and place in an ice bath to stop cooking. Drain and pat dry on paper towels. In the bowl of a food processor, combine the basil, cheese, pine nuts, garlic, salt and pepper. Purée on high speed. Slowly add the oil through the feed tube and process until a smooth paste forms.

CELERY ROOT PURÉE

3 large russet potatoes

sea salt and ground white pepper

1 large celery root

1 ½ cups heavy whipping cream

1 stick of butter, cut into pieces

Peel the potatoes and cut into 2" cubes. Place in a pot and cover with cold water. Add a generous amount of sea salt and bring to a boil over high heat. Cook until the potatoes are fork tender and drain in a colander. Meanwhile, peel the celery root and cut into 2" cubes. Place in a pot and cover with cold water. Add a generous amount of sea salt and bring to a boil over high heat. Cook until the celery root is fork tender and drain in a colander.

Bring the cream to a simmer over medium-high heat. Place the potatoes and celery root in a large kitchen towel and twist the towel to squeeze out as much water as possible. Put the potatoes and celery root in a food processor, add the cream and purée. Add the butter and purée again. Adjust seasoning to taste with salt and pepper.

FISH STOCK

4 pounds Fresh fish (*Red Snapper, Redfish, Speckled Trout, or Drum*)

1 gallon water

1 cup dry white wine

1 onion, peeled and sliced

1 stalk celery, sliced

1 carrot, peeled and chopped

4 cloves garlic, crushed with the side of a Chef's knife

2 tablespoons tomato paste

3 bay leaves

1 tablespoon fresh thyme

1 tablespoon dried oregano

stems from one bunch of fresh Italian parsley

3 tablespoons sea salt

2 tablespoons fresh ground black pepper

(tops of leeks and fennel are optional)

Fillet the fish, reserving the bones and meat separately. Place the bones in a large heavy bottomed stock pot and cover with the water. Place over high heat. Add the remaining ingredients and when it begins to boil, reduce the heat to a simmer. Simmer for one hour, skimming any impurities and foam that comes to the surface. Remove from heat and strain through a fine sieve. Discard the solids.

CHICKEN STOCK

2 chicken carcasses, from roasted or rotisserie chickens

1 onion, peeled and sliced

2 ribs of celery, sliced

1 large carrot, peeled and chopped

4 cloves of garlic, smashed

6 sprigs fresh thyme

2 sprigs fresh rosemary

1 tablespoon black peppercorns

1 tablespoon coriander seed

stems from 1 bunch of parsley

1 cup white wine

3 quarts chicken broth

Combine all of the ingredients in a large stockpot and set over medium-high heat. When it begins to boil, reduce the heat to a simmer and allow to cook for one hour. Skim off any oil and foam that rises to the top. Remove from heat and strain through a fine strainer discarding the solids. Return the stock to the pot and simmer until reduced to 2 quarts.

VODKA TOMATO
CREAM

MAYHAW
VINAIGRETTE

BÉCHAMEL
SAUCE

GREEN ONION
DIPPING SAUCE

BBQ SHRIMP
BUTTER

CHORON
SAUCE

HOLLANDAISE
SAUCE

SCLAFANI
DRESSING

RAVIGOTE
SAUCE

MUSTARD
SAUCE

VODKA TOMATO CREAM

2 ounces Vodka

2 ounces heavy whipping cream

4 ounces tomato basil sauce

2 tablespoons butter

2 tablespoons Romano cheese, grated

2 tablespoons Parmesan cheese, grated

1 tablespoon fresh basil, chiffonade

sea salt and fresh ground black pepper

Heat a sauté pan over medium high heat. Remove the pan from the heat and add the vodka carefully. Return to the heat. This should cause the vodka to ignite. When the flame subsides, add the cream and tomato basil sauce and bring to a boil. Reduce the heat to a simmer and add the butter while shaking or stirring the pan. Continue shaking the pan until the butter is incorporated. Remove from heat and add the cheeses and basil. Season with salt and pepper to taste.

MAYHAW VINAIGRETTE

1 cup Champagne vinegar

2 cups mayhaw jelly

3 cups olive oil

1 tablespoon garlic, minced

1 teaspoon sea salt

½ teaspoon fresh ground black pepper

Combine all ingredients and mix with an immersion blender.

BÉCHAMEL SAUCE

4 tablespoons butter

1 cup onion, peeled and chopped

½ tablespoon garlic, minced

1 bay leaf

2 cloves

1 teaspoon fresh thyme, chopped

4 tablespoons flour

1 quart milk

pinch nutmeg

1 teaspoon sea salt

½ teaspoon ground white pepper

In a saucepan, melt the butter over medium-high heat. Add the onion and cook for 5 minutes until softened. Add the garlic, bay leaf, clove and thyme and cook for 1 minute while stirring. Reduce the heat to medium and blend in the flour while stirring. Slowly stream in the milk while whisking. Bring to a simmer and cook for 5 minutes.

Strain through a fine mesh strainer. Season with nutmeg, salt, and pepper.

CARAMEL SAUCE

1 cup sugar

½ cup heavy whipping cream

Place the sugar in a heavy bottomed sauce pot, add ¼ cup water and bring to a boil. Cook, while whisking, until the sugar is dissolved and the consistency of syrup with a golden brown color. Remove from heat and carefully whisk in the heavy cream.

GREEN ONION DIPPING SAUCE

2 bunches green onions, chopped

½ cup fresh parsley sprigs

1 tablespoon chopped shallots

1 tablespoon chopped garlic

juice of one lime

2 large eggs

1 teaspoon sea salt

1 teaspoon fresh ground black pepper

1 ½ cups olive oil

Place the green onions, parsley, shallots, and garlic in a food processor or blender and purée. Add the eggs, salt, and pepper, and continue to process. With the machine running, stream in the olive oil slowly until it's thoroughly incorporated. Serve immediately.

BBQ SHRIMP BUTTER

1 pound butter, cut into chips, at room temperature

1 tablespoon fresh ground black pepper

2 tablespoons Creole seasoning (page 166)

3 tablespoons Worcestershire sauce

2 tablespoons garlic, chopped

juice of 1 ½ lemons

2 tablespoons fresh rosemary, minced

To make the compound butter, place the butter, black pepper, Creole seasoning, Worcestershire, garlic, lemon juice, and rosemary in a food processor. Blend until completely smooth and well blended.

Lay a sheet of plastic wrap on the counter and place the compound butter on the wrap and form into a log. Twist the ends to seal.

Refrigerate.

CHORON SAUCE

½ pound butter, melted

2 egg yolks

1 tablespoon hot water

juice of 1 lemon

1 ½ teaspoons sea salt

dash cayenne

dash Louisiana hot sauce

¼ cup tomato sauce

In a small stainless steel bowl, combine the yolks, hot water, lemon juice, salt, cayenne, and hot sauce. Place over a pot of boiling water and whisk vigorously. Be careful that your eggs don't scramble. The bowl should not get too hot too fast. Remove it from heat to control the temperature. When the mixture begins to get thick (the whisk pulls a ribbon through it) remove from heat. While whisking, add the melted butter a little at a time waiting until it is incorporated before adding more butter. If the mixture begins to break or get too thick, add a little hot water. Stir in the tomato sauce. Keep warm.

CREOLE REMOULADE

1 cups salad oil (vegetable oil)

1 egg

5 ounces ketchup

2 ounces Worcestershire

⅓ cup prepared horseradish

⅓ cup Creole mustard

2 teaspoons red wine vinegar

2 anchovy filets

1 teaspoon garlic

1 teaspoon sea salt

½ teaspoon fresh ground black pepper

pinch cayenne, ground

pinch crushed red pepper

Set the oil aside. Combine the remaining ingredients in a food processor and blend. Slowly add in the oil while blending.

MUSTARD SAUCE

1 tablespoon Colman's dry mustard

1 cups mayonnaise

2 teaspoons Worcestershire

1 teaspoon sea salt

½ teaspoon Tabasco

6 ounces Dijon mustard

½ tablespoons lemon juice

½ tablespoons A.1. steak sauce

Combine all ingredients together in a mixing bowl and blend well.

RAVIGOTE SAUCE

1 teaspoon dry mustard

1 tablespoon fresh lemon juice

1 cup mayonnaise

¼ cup of red bell pepper, seeded and minced

¼ cup of green bell pepper, seeded and minced

1 ½ tablespoons capers, drained and chopped

1 tablespoon fresh Italian parsley, minced

¼ cup Creole mustard

¼ cup prepared horseradish

½ teaspoon fresh ground black pepper

½ teaspoon tarragon, dried

1 teaspoon Louisiana hot sauce

1 teaspoon Worcestershire sauce

In a large mixing bowl, combine all the ingredients and mix well.

HOLLANDAISE SAUCE

½ pound butter, melted

2 egg yolks

1 tablespoon hot water

juice of 1 lemon

Louisiana hot sauce to taste

sea salt to taste

cayenne pepper to taste

Bring a sauce pot of water to a simmer. In a mixing bowl, whisk the egg yolks with hot water and lemon juice. Place the bowl over the simmering water and whisk constantly until the egg yolks are cooked and thickened. They should leave a ribbon when the whisk is pulled through. Remove the bowl from the water and whisk in the melted butter in a slow steady stream until all the butter is incorporated. Season with salt, pepper, and hot sauce. Keep warm until ready to use. Alternatively, you can make this in a blender. Bring the butter to a boil in a small saucepan. Meanwhile, in a blender, add the yolks, hot water, lemon juice, hot sauce, salt, and cayenne pepper. When the butter begins to boil, turn on the blender and slowly pour in the boiling butter in a slow steady stream. Turn off the blender and taste for seasoning. Keep warm.

CUMIN LIME CREMA

1 cup sour cream

juice of 1 lime

1 teaspoon cumin

1 teaspoon sea salt

½ teaspoon ground white pepper

In a small stainless steel mixing bowl, combine all the ingredients and whisk well. Store in the refrigerator until needed.

ACKNOWLEDGMENTS

When accomplishing such a large goal of producing a cookbook there are never too many cooks in the kitchen. It's with my colleagues, friends and family's amazing support that such a large project was brought to fruition.

I'd like to raise a glass to toast those who this wouldn't have been possible without.

First and foremost my amazing family. My wife Michelle has selflessly enabled me to follow my dream and to my children, Katherine and Peter. They are reason I wake up every morning and do what I do.

I'd like also like to toast:

My Grandfather, Peter Sclafani, Sr. for beginning our family's tradition of restaurants with the original Sclafani's Restaurant on Palmyra Street and then on Causeway Boulevard in Metairie.

My grandparents, Earl and Elise Stonecypher for teaching me to appreciate local, New Orleans cuisine and the importance of fresh, regional and home-grown ingredients with a story.

My parents, Peter Jr. and Jean Sclafani, for raising me in our family's restaurant, Sclafani's on Hayne Boulevard, in New Orleans. My upbringing in their restaurant planted the seed that has shaped the course of my life as a chef and restaurant owner.

My brother, Gino, Corporate Chef of Ruffino's Restaurant. He shares the same passion I do in the kitchen, and his love and support has helped me along the way. It's humbling to not only to be able to come to work every day to do something I love, but to also be able to work with my brother in the kitchen.

My business partner, Ruffin Rodrigue Jr., who is the perfect compliment to myself to run our family of restaurants. A great restaurateur and an even better friend. My former partner, TJ Moran, who expected more of me than I expected of myself, taught me a great deal about the business of the restaurant business.

As much as my family has played a major role in who I have become I would be remiss to not thank those great colleagues who were such a large part of this:

The Ruffino's Baton Rouge team - Howard Walker, Brandy Gabel, Ryan D'Arensbourg, Will Petty, Brad Morris, Daren Crawford, Mindy Walker and the entire staff.

The Ruffino's on the River Lafayette team - Kyle Waters III, Katie Gross, Nancy DeVille, Aaron Andre', Rene Schnell, Morgan Deshotels, Clayton Chauvin, and the entire staff.

The Xdesign team was such a large part of creating this book, especially Hunter Territo who helped put my words on paper and pushing me to make this dream a reality and Tiffanie Pitre for designing such a beautiful book and art directing the photo shoots which both far exceeded my expectations. I'd also like to thank a few other Xdesign team members; Jamey Crump, Christine Kennedy, John Gibby, and John Worrel for their great creative, design, proofing, editing, organizing, and scheduling support of all of our brands.

Our great photographers Collin Richie and Frank McMains who brought these wonderful recipes to life.

Our public relations team, Champion Management: Eric Spiritas and Ladd Biro.

Lastly and certainly not least, I'd like to offer a cheers to my friends that have supported me, my family and our restaurants throughout the years. They make this fun.

Mark and Leslie Culotta, Bill Hammack, Donald Link, Steve Stryjewski, Beau Box, Robert Schneckenberger, Jamie Beeman, Kathleen Wood, Todd Graves, Matt McKay, Chef John Folse, Mayor Kip Holden, John DeAngelo, Paul and Candi Ferachi, Cecile and Ruffin Rodrigue Sr., Sister Dulce Maria and Kim Johnson, Dr. Tom Kiebach and Beth Haynes, Art Favre, Lee Kantrow, and Bob Tucker.

RESOURCES

ANDOUILLE

Wayne Jacob's Smokehouse

769 West 5th Street

LaPlace, Louisiana 70068

(985) 652-9990

www.wjsmokehouse.com

BACON

**Benton's Smokey Mountain
Country Hams**

2603 Highway 411

Madisonville, Tennessee 37354

(423) 442-5003

www.bentonshams.com

CANE SYRUP AND
CANE VINEGAR

Steen's Cane Syrup

P.O. Box 339

119 North Main Street

Abbeville, Louisiana 70510

(800) 725-1654

www.steensyrup.com

CREOLE MUSTARD

Zatarain's

www.zatarains.com

EQUIPMENT

J.B. Prince Company

(800) 473-0577

www.jbprince.com

Williams-Sonoma

(800) 541-1262

www.williams-sonoma.com

OYSTERS

P&J Oyster Company

1039 Toulouse Street

New Orleans, Louisiana

(888) 522-2968

www.oysterlover.com

WILD GAME

D'Artagnan

(800) 327-8246

www.dartagnan.com

LOUISIANA SEAFOOD

New Orleans Fish House

921 South Dupre Street

New Orleans, Louisiana

(800) 839-3474

**Louisiana Seafood Promotion
& Marketing Board**

www.louisianaseafood.com

Crawfish Town USA Fresh Market

2815 - B Grand Point Highway

Breaux Bridge, Louisiana 70517

(337) 667-8888

KITCHEN MEASUREMENTS

LIQUID OR VOLUME MEASURES *(approximate)*			
1 teaspoon		⅓ tablespoon	5 ml
1 tablespoon	½ fluid ounce	3 teaspoons	15 ml (15 cc)
2 tablespoons	1 fluid ounce	⅛ cup, 6 teaspoons	30 ml (30 cc)
¼ cup	2 fluid ounces	4 tablespoons	59 ml
⅓ cup	2 ⅔ fluid ounces	5 tablespoons and 1 teaspoon	79 ml
½ cup	4 fluid ounces	8 tablespoons	118 ml
⅔ cup	5 ⅓ fluid ounces	10 tablespoons and 2 teaspoons	158 ml
¾ cup	6 fluid ounces	12 tablespoons	177 ml
⅞ cup	7 fluid ounces	14 tablespoons	207 ml
1 cup	8 fluid ounces (½ pint)	16 tablespoons	237 ml
2 cups	16 fluid ounces (1 pint)	32 tablespoons	473 ml
4 cups	32 fluid ounces	1 quart	946 ml
1 pint	16 fluid ounces (1 pint)	32 tablespoons	473 ml
2 pints	32 fluid ounces	1 quart	946 ml (0.946 liters)
8 pints	1 gallon (128 fluid ounces)	4 quarts	3785 ml (3.78 liters)
4 quarts	1 gallon (128 fluid ounces)	1 gallon	3785 ml (3.78 liters)
1 liter	1.057 quarts		1000 ml
1 gallon	4 quarts	128 fluid ounces	3785 ml (3.78 liters)
1 kilogram	2.2 pounds (35.2 ounces)	1000 gram	

Common ingredients and their approximate equivalents:

1 cup uncooked white rice = 185 grams

1 cup all-purpose flour = 140 grams

1 stick butter (4 ounces • 1/2 cup • 8 tablespoons) = 110 grams

1 cup butter (8 ounces • 2 sticks • 16 tablespoons) = 220 grams

1 cup brown sugar, firmly packed = 225 grams

1 cup granulated sugar = 200 grams

DRY OR WEIGHT MEASUREMENTS *(approximate)*		
1 ounce		30 grams (28.35 g)
2 ounces		55 grams
3 ounces		85 grams
4 ounces	¼ pound	125 grams
8 ounces	½ pound	240 grams
12 ounces	¾ pound	375 grams
16 ounces	1 pound	454 grams
32 ounces	2 pounds	907 grams
¼ pound	4 ounces	125 grams
½ pound	8 ounces	240 grams
¾ pound	12 ounces	375 grams
1 pound	16 ounces	454 grams
2 pounds	32 ounces	907 grams
1 kilogram	2.2 pounds (35.2 ounces)	1000 grams

INDEX